....

ARE YOU MY TYPE, AM I YOURS?

At the Movie Theater

ARE YOU MY TYPE, AM I YOURS?

Relationships Made Easy Through the Enneagram

Renee Baron &
Elizabeth Wagele

HarperSanFrancisco
An Imprint of HarperCollins*Publishers*

....

In gratitude to my friend and coauthor Elizabeth (a Five);
my family, Jodi, Tami, and Dan; and my friends and spiritual seekers
in the Twelve-Step community for their love and support.
—*Renee*

To my friend Renee (a Two); my family,
Gus, Nick/Michai, Martha/Steve, Augie, and Miranda/Ramy;
and my other friends.
—*Liz*

Text by Renee and Elizabeth
Drawings by Elizabeth

ARE YOU MY TYPE, AM I YOURS? *Relationships Made Easy Through the Enneagram.* Copyright © 1995 by Renee Baron and Elizabeth Wagele. All rights reserved. Printed in the United States of America. No part of this book may be used or re-produced in any manner whatsoever without written permission except in the case of brief quotations embodied in critical articles and reviews. For information address HarperCollins Publishers, 10 East 53rd Street, New York, NY 10022.

HarperCollins®, ▦ ®, and HarperSanFrancisco™ are trademarks of HarperCollins Publishers Inc.

FIRST EDITION

Library of Congress Cataloging-in-Publication Data
Baron, Renee.
Are you my type, am I yours? : relationships made easy through
the enneagram / Renee Baron & Elizabeth Wagele. — 1st ed.
p.   cm.
Includes bibliographical references.
ISBN 0–06–251248–X (pbk.)
1. Enneagram.   2. Interpersonal relations—Testing.
3. Typology (Psychology).   I. Wagele, Elizabeth.   II. Title.
BF698.35.E54B37   1995
155.2'6—dc20   95–14405
                                                                            CIP

96 97 98 99 ❖RRD(H) 10 9 8 7 6 5 4 3 2

CONTENTS

ABOUT THE

ENNEAGRAM AND RELATIONSHIPS

Humor is the shortest distance between two people.
—Victor Borge

Whether you are looking for a way to find the appropriate partner, to improve a relationship, or to understand people in general, you have come to the right place. You are about to meet the nine types of people as described by the Enneagram. One useful feature of the Enneagram is its ability to identify and explain various personality traits and preoccupations. Another is its teaching that we are not wrong for being different from one another.

The nine types might as well come from nine planets, judging from their varied motivations. Each has a different value system and different reality, brings something different to life, and wants something different out of life.

The Enneagram is symbolized by a nine-pointed star within a circle. *Ennea* means nine in Greek, and *gram* means a drawing. This symbol goes back hundreds of years to the Middle East. It was adapted to the study of personality types in the 1960s by a

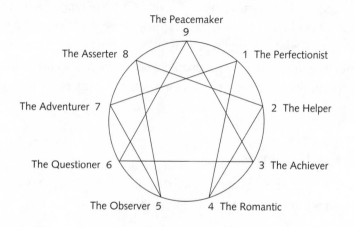

Bolivian psychiatrist, Oscar Ichazo, and by a Chilean psychiatrist, Claudio Naranjo. Enneagram teachers from varied disciplines have added to its development through their writings and by organizing classes where students can listen to examples of the nine types speak.

The Enneagram can give you tools to help you change and grow, choose a partner wisely, or bring a troubled relationship back to life.

The first task in learning about the nine types is to find out which type you are. The second task is to learn to see the other eight types as they see themselves.

The Three Centers

Finding your "center" is a starting place for finding your type. Each center corresponds to a part of the body: the heart (types Two, Three, and Four), the head (types Five, Six, and Seven), and the gut (types Eight, Nine, and One). While you may be able to communicate more easily with people who are in your center, close relationships with people in the other centers can help bring the elements of your personality into balance.

The Heart Center Types

These types are concerned with making heart connections. Since they focus on how others see them, they are sometimes out of touch with their real feelings.

Helpers (Twos)
are interested in
people, play the role
of nurturer, and try
to present a loving
image.

Achievers (Threes)
try to be seen in a
good light, according
to socially agreed-
upon norms.

Romantics (Fours)
have a strong need to
express themselves
and to be seen as
original.

The Head or Thinking Center Types

Each of these types has a different way of dealing with fear.

Observers (Fives)
rely on their own re-
sources and find safety
in knowledge and/or
withdrawing.

Questioners (Sixes)
try to control their fear
through vigilance,
approval of authority
figures, or through re-
belling against authority.

Adventurers (Sevens)
are active and opti-
mistic. They avoid un-
pleasant emotions,
including fear.

The Gut Center Types

These types have issues that revolve around self-forgetting and anger.

Asserters (Eights) are powerful and not afraid to express their anger.

Peacemakers (Nines) are accommodating and are often out of touch with their anger.

Perfectionists (Ones) see anger as a character flaw and repress it.

One of the Enneagram's goals is to teach you to observe and harmonize all three centers within yourself.

Wings and Arrows

Your personality is influenced by the types or numbers next to yours, the *wings*. It is also influenced by the two numbers that are connected to yours by lines, the *arrows*.

In order to make changes and to grow, we can try to incorporate the positive traits of the wings and arrows into our personality and heal the negative ones. There remain four other types that we normally have less access to, unless we have been exposed to them through a parent or other significant person in our life. The aim is to take the healthy aspects of all nine types into ourselves in a continual process of growth and renewal.

After establishing which center is yours, you can start to narrow in on your individual type by filling out the personality inventories at the beginning of each chapter. Your type will probably be one of the two or three you score highest on, not necessarily your highest score.

It is best to read every chapter before you determine your type.

Subtypes

Each type has three subtypes, based on the three basic instincts required for life: *self-preservation* (survival or well-being), *relational* (one-to-one relationships; some Enneagram authors use the word *sexual* for this subtype), and *social* (how we relate to the community and the world at large). Ideally these instincts come into play spontaneously and are appropriate to the situation. As personality develops, however, one or more of these becomes distorted or exaggerated, and our behavior loses much of its flexibility. We can try to regain flexibility by first recognizing the form our subtypes take and then by making an effort to bring them back into balance with one another.

Normally we tend to ignore the way our subtypes manifest, and they push us around without our knowledge. Learning to observe and identify them can lead to tremendous self-awareness and growth. Studying the subtypes has helped many involved in the Twelve-Step community to pinpoint their strengths and shortcomings.

Self-preservation subtypes focus on well-being and self-sufficiency and are usually rather reserved and cautious. They are concerned about things related to the home and may have a tendency to hoard. They muster their own resources when in crisis. Some of this subtype challenge their need for security by being daring or dauntless, although most work on being safe.

Relational subtypes go toward other people and are usually intense, energetic, and competitive. They make direct eye contact as they strive to establish a personal connection. When in a group, the most important thing for them is to be noticed or loved by a specific person

there. Some deem it important to challenge their concern for another and therefore avoid involvement with other people.

Social subtypes either get energized by groups or dislike and avoid them. Those who relate positively to groups enjoy shared efforts, are concerned about what others are doing, and feel larger by identifying with world issues, principles, and justice.

Often Asked Questions

Are we born our type? We believe that inborn characteristics lead to the development of our Enneagram type. We use and overuse these traits as we form a personality and develop a strategy for coping with life. In doing so, we shut out the possibility of developing contrasting traits. For instance, a person who is competitive and aggressive in meeting goals cannot at the same time daydream and accept life as it comes.

Do people ever change types? No, but we can become healthier. In order to do this, we try to become less stuck in our limited way of being and open ourselves to the healthy traits and attitudes of all nine types.

Are any types better or worse than others? No.

I relate to so many Enneagram numbers. Can't I be more than one type? You have traits in common with all the numbers, but the underlying motivation of each type is different. This is the key to the Enneagram.

You will become more flexible and act appropriately in a wider range of situations as you grow using the Enneagram, but you always retain your basic style and motivation.

Do certain types get along better than other types? Yes, in a general way, but this isn't nearly as important as finding someone who

- you really like and respect and who really likes and respects you

- is psychologically healthy, doesn't withdraw, and is willing to work on problems

The Myers-Briggs Type Indicator

Many of the variations within the nine types can be explained by relating them to the highly respected Myers-Briggs Type Indicator (the MBTI). This test is based on the personality typology of Carl G. Jung. It is believed that we are born with a preference for four of the eight personality traits that the MBTI measures. These traits combine with the Enneagram and innumerable other factors to make us who we are.

The four MBTI scales are

Extroversion or Introversion—whether people relate more to the external or their internal world

Sensing or iNtuition—whether people take in or perceive information more through their five senses or through possibilities and hunches

Thinking or Feeling—whether people make evaluations and judgments using their head more or their heart

Judging or Perceiving—whether people live more in an organized way and seek closure or live in a spontaneous and open way

Each four-letter type consists of a combination of one preference from each of the above pairs of traits. For example, a person who prefers Introversion, iNtuition, Feeling, and Perceiving is referred to as an INFP.

The Myers-Briggs types are explained in the chapter beginning on page 158. This will probably give you a good idea of your MBTI type. If you wish to explore this further, most career counseling centers and many therapists are qualified to administer the MBTI test. In the back of this book there are charts that compare the two systems.

THE

PERFECTIONIST

Let my conscience be your guide.

Ones are motivated by the need to improve themselves and to live the right way.

While Ones are usually fastidious, some are more concerned with political, religious, or ethical principles than they are with physical neatness.

Eights, Nines, and Ones constitute the gut center and have issues that revolve around self-forgetting and anger. Ones follow the rules. They come to feel angry about their own self-imposed restrictions and the fact that others seem free to do as they please.

Ones at Their BEST Are	Ones at Their WORST Are
ethical	judgmental
idealistic	inflexible
productive	controlling
reliable	worrying
fair	argumentative
honest	nit-picking
self-disciplined	uncompromising
conscientious	stubborn
helpful	overly serious
objective	critical of others

Personality Inventory

Check what applies to you.

- ☐ 1 I demonstrate my love through effort and hard work.
- ☐ 2 I like to have everything orderly and in its place.
- ☐ 3 Completing a task gives me great pleasure.
- ☐ 4 I frequently do more than my fair share.
- ☐ 5 People who are sloppy about their work irritate me.
- ☐ 6 I don't like being judgmental, but it is hard not to be.
- ☐ 7 I focus on things that are wrong or out of order and how to fix them.
- ☐ 8 I tend to be serious and worry a lot.
- ☐ 9 I am very concerned with financial security.
- ☐ 10 You can always rely on me.
- ☐ 11 I am so used to struggling to better myself that I tend to discount whatever comes easily to me.
- ☐ 12 In order to avoid criticism from myself and others, I try to do everything correctly.
- ☐ 13 When others don't meet my expectations or do their part, I feel disappointed or offended.
- ☐ 14 I try hard not to let my jealous or angry feelings show when I have them.
- ☐ 15 I feel strongly about my principles and beliefs.
- ☐ 16 I carefully plan my day to be sure I get everything done.
- ☐ 17 It is difficult for me to forgive when I have been wronged.
- ☐ 18 I am reasonable, practical, and down-to-earth.
- ☐ 19 I continually look for ways to be a better person.
- ☐ 20 I am less likely to feel critical when I see that people are trying to reform.

Which Subtype Applies to You?

You May Relate to One, Two, or All Three Subtypes

Within each type there are three subtypes, representing the three aspects of instinctual life: personal well-being (*self-preservation*), one-to-one relationships (*relational*), and community (*social*). These subtypes or instincts are largely expressed in unconscious ways as we go about life. For most of us, the importance of one or more subtypes is exaggerated, though, and this interferes with our growth.

Ones cope with or divert attention from their anger in the following ways, according to their subtype. As they develop, they will move beyond these limitations, and their preoccupation with looking for flaws will become less dominant. They will begin to accept life as it is.

Self-Preservation Ones: "Worried and Anxious"

- Hardly a minute goes by when I'm not worrying about something: my finances, job security, the condition of the world, or little things such as what to buy for dinner.

- Changes in routine make me anxious.

- I may stay in an inappropriate or unsatisfying job for years rather than undergo the anxiety of looking for something new that I might like.

- I feel as if one error could ruin everything.

- I assess every last detail in advance in order to keep my life perfect and under control. When I finish worrying about myself, I worry about whether my loved ones are going to be safe and sound.

- I often imagine that someone is checking up on me or scrutinizing and criticizing everything I do.

- I frequently compare myself to other people, correct myself a lot, and apologize—or feel that I should apologize.

11

- Sometimes I procrastinate because I'm afraid to make a mistake.

Relational Ones: "Insecure and Jealous"

My wife's jealousy is getting ridiculous.
The other day she looked at my calendar and
demanded to know who May was.

—Rodney Dangerfield

- I tend to be overly possessive.

- I worry that my loved one will reject me for a more attractive or perfect person.

- I obsessively compare myself with others.

- When my partner or friend makes a positive comment about another person, such as, "He is a great cook," I get upset and think she means I am not a great cook.

- I feel ashamed and insecure when I experience boiling anger or jealousy. Sometimes I act overly enthusiastic or positive to cover up the feelings I think are improper.

- I become indignant when someone who doesn't deserve it gets honored or promoted or doesn't have to worry as much as I do about earning a living.

- I like the intensity of being fully and passionately engaged with another person.

- I try to get my partner to meet my high standards and expectations in order to make him or her—and our life together—better.

Social Ones: "Adaptable or Unadaptable"

- Sometimes I defend what I believe in so adamantly, it puts me on the outs with people.

- There are times when I really want to reform something or someone, but I quietly simmer rather than rock the boat. It's important to try to get along.

- I've been accused of being unyielding, but I deliberate carefully and thoroughly in forming my opinions and can see no reason to change them.

- I believe in cooperation, but I will not go along with anything that is completely against my principles.

- When people don't perform up to my standards, I feel I must set them straight.

- I am drawn to groups that share my ideals, but sometimes I end up overworking because the others don't get things done right. I often feel resentful and have to leave.

Feeling-type Ones try to be adaptable but aren't always able to be. Thinking-type Ones tend to be inadaptable and argumentative.

Wings

Wings are the types on each side of your number. When Ones lean toward their Nine wing, they are relatively detached. When Ones lean toward their Two wing, they tend to express feelings more.

Ones with a strong Nine wing tend to be easygoing, objective, moderate, impersonal, and stubborn.

Ones with a strong Two wing tend to be helpful, empathic, sensitive to others, image conscious, attention seeking, and controlling.

Occasionally people present the persona of one of their wings—rather than their actual type—to the outside world.

Arrows

Your personality is also influenced by the two types that are connected to yours by lines, the *arrows* of Four and Seven.

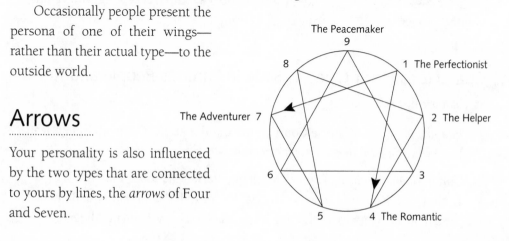

The Peacemaker
9

8

1 The Perfectionist

The Adventurer 7

2 The Helper

6

3

5

4 The Romantic

How Wings and Arrows Influence
Your Behavior in Relationships

We have a natural connection to our wings and arrows. They come into play without our knowing it: their positive aspects when we're feeling tranquil and integrated, and their unhealthy aspects during times of stress. When we want to change something about ourselves, we can try consciously to incorporate their favorable and avoid their negative traits. You may want to read the chapters on Nines, Twos, Fours, and Sevens to learn more about them.

Both wings of the One have a softening effect on this sometimes uptight personality. If you want to be less serious and rigid, emulate the calm and mellow traits of your Nine wing. Try to avoid the Nine's stubbornness, however. Your Two wing can help you express warmth, caring, and enthusiasm. But avoid putting a guilt trip on your partner for not taking your advice.

Emulate your Seven arrow to lighten up, to be more generous and spontaneous, and to have more fun. On the negative side, your Seven arrow can influence you to eat or drink excessively, use drugs, or do other dangerous activities.

Your Four arrow can have a very different effect on your personality by helping you turn inward, get in touch with deeper feelings, and use your creativity. On the down side of this arrow, you may feel hopeless or unlovable when you or your partner does not live up to your expectations.

Ones at their best accomplish a lot and find wise and fair solutions to problems. When healthy, they are realistic, understanding, accepting, and can have a terrific sense of humor.

Characteristics of Ones as Seen in Famous People and Roles

Speculations by the Authors

Fair and objective: Supreme Court Justice Sandra Day O'Conner, Captain Jean-Luc Picard of *Star Trek, the Next Generation*

Principled and idealistic: Thomas Jefferson, Nelson Mandela, Florence Nightingale, William F. Buckley, Jr., Atticus in *To Kill a Mockingbird*, Barbara Jordan, Mario Cuomo, Aleksandr Solzhenitsyn, Harry Truman, Margaret

Thatcher, Stevie Wonder (put his career on hold to be politically active and help make Martin Luther King, Jr.'s birthday a national holiday)

Fussy, finicky, or proper: Judith Martin (Miss Manners), Felix Unger in *The Odd Couple*, Mary Poppins, Dana Carvey's "church lady," Emily Post

Fiery or intense: Tina Turner, John Bradshaw

Clear and elegant: Johann Sebastian Bach

Classy and precise: Fred Astaire

Dedicated to change: Martin Luther, Ralph Nader, Dr. Jack Kevorkian, Cesar Chavez

Famous Pairs

One and One: George and Martha Washington

One and Two: Al and Tipper Gore

One and Three: William Holden and Faye Dunaway in *Network*

One and Four: Katharine Hepburn and Spencer Tracy

One and Five: Joanne Woodward and Paul Newman

One and Six: Arthur Miller and Marilyn Monroe

One and Seven: Emma Thompson and Kenneth Branagh

One and Eight: Tina and Ike Turner

One and Nine: Gene Siskel and Roger Ebert, film critics

Perfectionists in Relationships

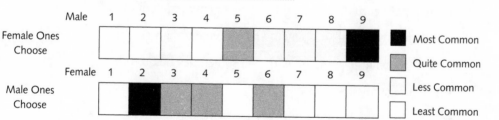

If a task is once begun
Never leave it 'til it's done.
Be the labor great or small
Do it well or not at all.

      —Anonymous

What Ones Say About Ones

I like Ones because we

- both have high ideals

- value each other's achievements

- value and put energy into being good family and community members

- enjoy each other's sense of humor

- do what we say we will do and take our share of the household responsibilities

I have trouble with Ones because we

- each think there is only one way to do everything

- reinforce each other's worries

- can be overly serious

- communicate censure and resentment through silence or glaring looks

- are too busy to have time to relax with each other

What Ones Say About Twos (Helpers)

I like Twos because they

- like to help me and appreciate what I do for them

- are good-hearted, warm, and give me plenty of attention

- are often youthful and playful and help me to lighten up

- perceive what is going on with me, sometimes before I do

- encourage my best qualities

- take charge of planning our social activities

I have trouble with Twos because they

- become hurt at the slightest criticism

- want more attention than I can give them

- don't always think things through methodically

- sometimes neglect to examine the consequences of their actions

- give in to people in order to be liked

- seem always to want to talk about our relationship

What Ones Say About Threes (Achievers)

I like Threes because they

- work hard and accomplish a lot, as I do

- teach me how to focus on the positive

- are good at moving things along efficiently

- engage in lively discussions with me

- usually look sharp and blend into most social situations

I have trouble with Threes because they

- offend me when they try to impress people and brag about their accomplishments

- are overly sensitive to criticism and withdraw when confronted

- don't care about getting things done perfectly
- tend to put their work ahead of family responsibilities

What Ones Say About Fours (Romantics)

I like Fours because they

- are honest about their feelings and help me get in touch with mine
- can be playful, witty, and charming
- have good analytical abilities (especially those with a strong Five wing)
- are highly principled and idealistic
- are compassionate and supportive

I have trouble with Fours because they

- brood, become hurt easily, and feel sorry for themselves
- process their feelings endlessly
- put off doing what they should do until they are in just the right mood
- can be self-centered
- demand too much attention

What Ones Say About Fives (Observers)

I like Fives because they

- are interesting and bright
- speak with sincerity, depth, and substance
- are wise and give me good advice
- stay with tasks until they're completed
- are thrifty, moral, and nonjudgmental
- don't make excessive demands on my time

I have trouble with Fives because they

- resist going to functions I consider obligatory

- become quarrelsome when I challenge their logic or disagree with them

- often have a slower pace than I do and try my patience

- become silent and withdraw instead of working things out with me

What Ones Say About Sixes (Questioners)

I like Sixes because they

- are warm, supportive, and compassionate (especially the self-preservation subtypes)

- are reliable and hardworking

- have a strong sense of duty

- work diligently for the causes they believe in

- support me through difficult times

I have trouble with Sixes because they

- lash out angrily at me and make sarcastic or blaming remarks (especially when counterphobic)

- worry even more than I do

- can be volatile, erratic, and controlling

- procrastinate

What Ones Say About Sevens (Adventurers)

I like Sevens because they

- seek new knowledge and experiences as eagerly as I seek new ways to improve myself

- show me what it's like to be flexible and spontaneous

- are idealistic and want to better the world, as I do

- don't let setbacks and disappointments get them down

- are free spirits and can show me how to enjoy life

I have trouble with Sevens because they

- can be self-centered

- are always in a hurry and won't take time to listen to me and my worries

- get critical, defensive, and self-righteous

- don't prioritize or follow rules as much as I think they should

- should think things through more carefully before they do things

What Ones Say About Eights (Asserters)

I like Eights because they

- are bigger than life and not as constricted as I am

- are enthusiastic and dynamic—we can be an electric combination

- take the initiative when they want something to be done

- encourage me to go after my goals more aggressively

- stand up courageously for what they believe in

- encourage me to express my anger

I have trouble with Eights because they

- do things to excess instead of practicing moderation

- feel no guilt or remorse when they hurt my feelings

- can be uncouth and embarrass me

- get into vicious fights with me

- refuse to see things my way

What Ones Say About Nines (Peacemakers)

I like Nines because they

- are accepting and influence me to accept myself more

- don't threaten or try to manipulate me

- are understanding and nonjudgmental

- have a broad view and help me put things in perspective

- encourage me to take it easy and enjoy myself

I have trouble with Nines because they

- drive me crazy when they get slow, stubborn, or indecisive

- get vague or float off and daydream when I try to talk about important matters

- sometimes live vicariously through me or others

- minimize problems and hope they will go away instead of fixing them

The calmest husbands make the stormiest wives.

   —Isaac Disraeli

Things Ones Would Never Dream of Doing . . .

☞ letting their spouse wear a sweatsuit to their twenty-fifth high school reunion

☞ not checking to see if they got back the correct change

☞ telling guests to bring all the food and drinks to their party, since they're planning to be tied up at the beach all day

☞ not lifting a finger to help when visiting their fiancé as he recovers from surgery

> Bring -- bedpan -- please ...

> I can't. My nails are wet.

☞ not feeling the least pang of jealousy when their partner talks in glowing terms about a new co-worker of the opposite sex

☞ slurping their drink with their straw at a power business lunch

☞ taking it in stride when the meal they cook for their in-laws or boss burns

How to Get Along with Ones

- Appreciate their ethics, high standards, and the steadiness and security they bring to your relationship.

- Show them that you are a trustworthy and loyal partner.

- Praise them for their concern for others and for being helpful.

- Show your appreciation by giving them cards, gifts, or hugs.

- Admit mistakes. Ones love it when people feel remorse.

- When in conflict, show them you are looking for a way to resolve the matter constructively.

- Do your share of the chores and household responsibilities. Ones want things to be fair.

- Always use your best manners.

- Keep things orderly and organized and be on time.

- Keep in mind that Ones, especially feeling types, pick up the slightest negative remarks—ones that others would not even be aware of.

- Be gentle and sensitive when registering complaints.

- If necessary, tell them that praise and encouragement will get better results from you than criticism.

You can give Ones extra support in these ways:

- Reassure them that they have no need to prove they are perfect.

- Remind them that you still love them when they express their anger. If they trust you enough to have a healthy argument or fight, this will relieve a lot of their tension.

- Show understanding if they make a mistake.

- Take them on a vacation. Ones lighten up dramatically when away from home and responsibility.

- Encourage them to schedule time for relaxation and enjoyment.

THE

HELPER

If you want to be loved, be lovable.

—Ovid

Twos are motivated by the need to be loved and valued and to express their positive feelings toward others.

Twos are prone to being codependent, though codependency is found in all the types.

Twos, Threes, and Fours constitute the heart center of the Enneagram and focus on their image or how others see them. Twos want to make a difference in people's lives and want to be seen as likable, upbeat, and attentive.

Twos at Their BEST Are	Twos at Their WORST Are
loving	indirect
warm	overly accommodating
adaptable	overly demonstrative (the more extroverted Twos)
generous	
enthusiastic	controlling
attentive	possessive
appreciative	insincere
perceptive	martyrlike
expressive	manipulative
friendly	hysterical

Personality Inventory

Check what applies to you.

- [ ] 1 I have a warm and friendly personality.
- [ ] 2 I pay people compliments to reassure them and let them know they are special to me.
- [ ] 3 It is difficult for me to ask for what I need, or even to know what it is, when I'm with others.
- [ ] 4 I like to receive approval, respect, recognition, and admiration.
- [ ] 5 People enjoy my enthusiastic and optimistic attitude.
- [ ] 6 It is difficult for me to express my negative feelings directly to someone, but I may complain to others about him or her.
- [ ] 7 I suffer terribly when disregarded or taken for granted, and I punish the offender subtly or sneakily.
- [ ] 8 It is usually more comfortable for me to give than to receive.
- [ ] 9 I like to reach out to people and often am the one to make the first overture.
- [ ] 10 I have become exhausted or ill from taking care of others.
- [ ] 11 I usually hold eye contact and listen attentively in conversations.
- [ ] 12 Some people see me as overly emotional and dramatic.
- [ ] 13 I can be taken for granted and not be aware of it.
- [ ] 14 I sometimes feel a deep sense of loneliness.
- [ ] 15 When I feel needy and vulnerable, I try not to show it.
- [ ] 16 People feel comfortable revealing their problems to me.
- [ ] 17 I usually know what other people need and what they are feeling.
- [ ] 18 I know how to get people to like me.
- [ ] 19 Sometimes I feel trapped and angry with myself when I realize I have given up my own interests for another's.
- [ ] 20 I like feeling indispensable and helping others become more successful.

Which Subtype Applies to You?

You May Relate to One, Two, or All Three Subtypes

Within each type there are three subtypes, representing the three aspects of instinctual life: personal well-being (*self-preservation*), one-to-one relationships (*relational*), and community (*social*). These subtypes or instincts are largely expressed in unconscious ways as we go about life. For most of us, the importance of one or more subtypes is exaggerated, though, and interferes with our growth.

Twos cope with their need to lose themselves in another in the following ways, depending on their subtype. As they develop, they will be less dependent on the admiration and approval of others to feel worthwhile.

Self-Preservation Twos: "Deserving of Privileges"

- If I don't receive cards, gifts, or other signs of appreciation for being giving, devoted, and self-sacrificing, I feel devastated, hurt, and angry.

- I like to pamper myself. I often indulge in wonderful food treats, shopping excursions, special vacations, or other luxuries.

- I often spend more than I need to, but I can always justify it.

- I look for someone to support me financially and/or emotionally.

- I often feel young and needy but cover it up by acting helpful and strong.

- Helping my partner achieve his or her potential is gratifying and makes me feel important. It also spares *me* the risk of failure.

- Sometimes I feel I deserve preferential treatment because of all the things I have done for others.

Relational Twos: "Persistent and Seductive"

- I go after what I want. This applies to relationships as well as to other areas of my life.

- If I don't reach out to people, I feel that I may be overlooked or forgotten.

- I have perfected many skills to lure people I'm romantically interested in. I alter my personality, dress attractively, turn on charm, learn their likes and dislikes, and listen attentively to their every word.

- I long to have a close relationship, but I know from experience that I can lose myself this way.

- I often choose inappropriate or unavailable people, as this keeps me from having to face my fears of intimacy.

- I sometimes choose a partner I plan to improve, change, or bring out.

- I like the chase! I hook someone in and *then* discover if I like her or him.

Social Twos: "Ambitious"

*To love one that is great
is almost to be great oneself.*

—Suzanne Curchod

- I like to make a difference in people's lives.

- I seek important roles; I like to be the leader or assistant to a powerful leader.

- Highly visible work can make me anxious because of the possibility I'll be embarrassed if I should fail in some way.

- I strive to be recognized and valued for my warmth, friendliness, and expertise.

- I try to seek approval by being charming, upbeat, competent, energetic, and by entertaining graciously in my home.

- I love getting compliments like, "I couldn't have done it without you."

- I'm ambitious for my partner and boss, but I resent their success when I have done much of their work.

Wings

Wings are the types on each side of yours. When Twos lean toward their Three wing, they are even more invested in their image. When Twos lean toward their One wing, they tend to focus on doing things properly.

Twos with a strong One wing tend to be principled, altruistic, objective, guilt ridden, self-critical, controlling, self-righteous, and judgmental and are more likely to be introverted. Twos with a strong Three wing tend to be sociable, self-assured, ambitious, competitive, vain, manipulative, deceptive, and are more likely to be extroverted.

People sometimes present the persona of one of their wings—rather than their actual type—to the outside world.

Arrows

Your personality is also influenced by the two types that are connected to yours by lines, the *arrows* of Four and Eight.

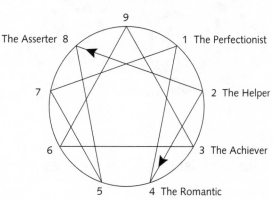

How Wings and Arrows Influence Your Behavior in Relationships

We have a natural connection to our wings and arrows. They come into play without our knowing it: their positive aspects when we're feeling tranquil and integrated, and their unhealthy aspects during times of stress. When we want to change something about ourselves, we can try consciously to incorporate their favorable and avoid their negative traits. You may want to read the chapters on Ones, Threes, Fours, and Eights to learn more about them.

Twos are sandwiched between very efficient wings. The One wing can add order, clarity, objectivity, and idealism to your personality. Be aware of One's judgmental, moralistic, and pessimistic aspects. Your Three wing will help you to be more energetic, purposeful, and optimistic. Avoid emulating the Three's negative tendencies to be self-centered, exploitive, or overly competitive.

Going toward your Four arrow can bring out your creative potential and help you learn to feel and express the full range of your emotions, not just your loving ones. You can also learn to be more honest, to discover other sources of self-worth besides helping, and to enjoy your own company more. Be aware of the Four's envy and self-absorption, however.

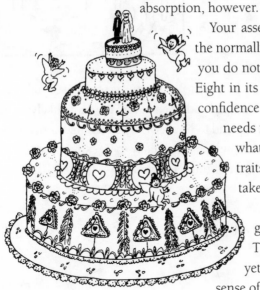

Your assertive Eight arrow is a big contrast to the normally helpful Two and may come out when you do not feel appreciated. You can emulate the Eight in its more positive aspect to develop more confidence and strength, to express your own needs more straightforwardly, and to go after what you want directly. Avoid the Eight's traits of attacking, blaming, and tending to take charge of everyone and everything.

Twos at their healthiest are warm, generous, empathic, and compassionate. They make great partners and friends, yet they maintain their own interests and sense of self.

Characteristics of Twos as Seen in Famous People and Roles

Speculations by the Authors

Compassionate: Mother Teresa, Virginia Satir (the mother of family therapy)

Friendly, caring, and warm: Ellen Burstyn, Alan Alda, Dr. T. Berry Brazelton, Sammy Davis, Jr., Sally Jessy Raphael

Charitable: Danny Glover, Sophia Loren, Elizabeth Taylor

Spreading love: Leo Buscaglia, Rev. Cecil Williams of San Francisco's Glide Memorial Church

Seductive: Marilyn Monroe in *Gentlemen Prefer Blondes,* Madonna, Rita Hayworth

Idealistic: Betty Friedan, Bishop Desmond Tutu

Image conscious: Imelda Marcos, Susan Powter

Advice-giving: columnist Ann Landers, psychologist Joyce Brothers

Addicted to love: Glenn Close in *Fatal Attraction,* Rebecca on *Cheers*

Strong partner: Barbara Bush ("I am nothing without George Bush"), Nancy Reagan

Famous Pairs

Two and One:	Alice B. Toklas and Gertrude Stein
Two and Two:	The Huxtables on *The Cosby Show*
Two and Three:	Elvis and Priscilla Presley
Two and Four:	Jessica Lange and Sam Shepard
Two and Five:	Jessica Walter and Clint Eastwood in *Play Misty for Me*
Two and Six:	Marlo Thomas and Phil Donahue
Two and Seven:	Kathie Lee Gifford and Regis Philbin, co-hosts
Two and Eight:	Elizabeth Taylor and Richard Burton
Two and Nine:	Nancy and Ronald Reagan

Helpers in Relationships

There is no greater experience than to be wanted.

—Moondog, New York street poet

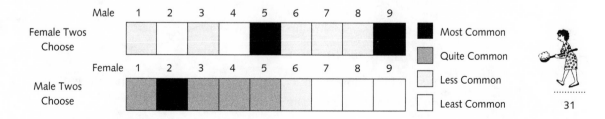

What Twos Say About Ones (Perfectionists)

I like Ones because they

- give me a sense of security by being definite, steady, and trustworthy
- always keep their word
- take care of practical details
- have a strong sense of duty and responsibility to the community
- want to make the world a better place
- appreciate my ability to relate to people

I have trouble with Ones because they

- criticize me for not measuring up to their standards and leave me feeling inadequate, hurt, and angry
- can treat people harshly and hold onto grudges
- do not express the loving feelings toward me that I need

- work too much and can't find time to play
- are very, very careful of their money

What Twos Say About Twos

I like Twos because we

- are tuned in to each other
- enjoy being together
- give each other a sense of really being loved and appreciated
- both value family and friends
- have many of the same interests, including liking to discuss people and relationships and liking the same movies, plays, and books

I have trouble with Twos because we

- find it hard to be honest and direct with each other

- get hurt easily and are very sensitive to criticism

- often can't decide where to go or what to do when we're together

- compete with each other for attention

- both can flirt and make the other jealous

What Twos Say About Threes (Achievers)

I like Threes because they

- are energetic, optimistic, and upbeat

- are usually successful

- make a good impression

- mix well in different kinds of groups

- give me a sense of freedom by not pulling at me to be responsible for them

I have trouble with Threes because they

- can be overly sensitive to criticism

- get defensive when I try to discuss problems with our relationship

- can be self-important and boast

- can be so involved in leaving their mark that they neglect their personal life; they seem to be married to their work

What Twos Say About Fours (Romantics)

I like Fours because they

- are compassionate and warm

- perceive and value my best qualities

- share their rich inner life with me

- can be extremely funny

- have a unique sense of style and aesthetics

I have trouble with Fours because they

- don't like to be with people as much as I do, especially introverted Fours

- have a push-pull habit in relationships (similar to my own)

- act superior and can be angry, biting, and overreactive

- can lose their grip on reality, wallow in their feelings, and be depressing to be around

What Twos Say About Fives (Observers)

I like Fives because they

- have an appealing, understated sense of humor

- listen well and give me constructive feedback

- like to touch and be close

- have the ability, which I lack, to be independent, objective, and detached

- are calm, quiet, and steady

- influence me to be more inner-directed

I have trouble with Fives because they

- get wrapped up in their projects or studies and don't give me enough attention

- withdraw and leave me feeling hurt and abandoned

- are often too abstract

- look down on me for being too emotional

- are usually too quiet and try to avoid parties and socializing

What Twos Say About Sixes (Questioners)

I like Sixes because they

- respect me when I express my feelings honestly
- have a good sense of humor
- are conscientious, loyal, and responsible
- care about the underdog and the unfortunate
- let me know that I can always lean on them

I have trouble with Sixes because they

- get on my nerves analyzing, theorizing, fretting, and obsessing
- always think I want something from them when I compliment or flatter them
- are often negative and erratic
- test, tease, and use sarcasm

What Twos Say About Sevens (Adventurers)

I like Sevens because they

- are sociable and enjoy life to the fullest
- give me freedom to do my own activities
- have many abilities and talents that make me proud of them
- appreciate the interest I take in their hopes, dreams, and plans
- are lovable, charming, and keep me interested in them

I have trouble with Sevens because they

- embarrass and bore me by monopolizing conversations and talking about themselves

- can make my head spin with their mental energy
- give me the sense of not being important when they neglect to consult or inform me
- ignore problems in the relationship, even after I point them out
- can become negative and unmovable

What Twos Say About Eights (Asserters)

I like Eights because they

- put energy and passion into living
- are powerful yet can be as tender as a teddy bear in an intimate relationship
- are earthy and love to be close physically
- give me the sense that I am trusted and special
- appreciate my ability to be a good listener
- protect and encourage me
- know what they want and speak their minds

*Don't tell me what
kind of day to have.*

        —seen on an Eight's T-shirt

I have trouble with Eights because they

- can be too possessive, demanding, and abusive
- are controlling, judgmental, and dominating
- put me on edge in social situations; I worry that they're going to act inappropriately or crudely or talk too much about themselves
- are often unaware of my and others' feelings and needs
- activate my worst fears about being weak and unable to stand up for myself

What Twos Say About Nines (Peacemakers)

I like Nines because they

- comfort me, reassure me, and make me feel loved and special

- enjoy being close and intimate

- are good listeners

- often put my welfare before their own

- appreciate my accomplishments and the things I do for them

- are gentle and kind

I have trouble with Nines because they

- act passive-aggressively instead of saying no directly

- are too apathetic, indecisive, and lacking in motivation

- don't always carry their share of the responsibility

- punish me by withdrawing and giving me the silent treatment

- pay more attention to their habits and activities than they do to me, especially when they're angry

Things Twos Would Never Dream of Doing . . .

☞ showing up at the potluck dinner empty-handed

☞ not fantasizing about controlling their partner's entire wardrobe

☞ not telling their friends, who have just had their home redecorated, what wonderful taste they have

☞ receiving the Mother Teresa Compassionate Citizen Award and not mentioning it

☞ going to their boyfriend's parents' house for the first time and not making one flattering remark

☞ typing their name, instead of signing it, on a birthday card to their boyfriend or girlfriend and not adding a syrupy message

☞ saying no when someone asks them to do a small favor

☞ not hoping the person who had rejected them would beg to be taken back

☞ resolving to use the Enneagram to change only themselves and not offering one suggestion to anyone else

How to Get Along with Twos

- Appreciate their warmth, generosity, enthusiasm, and sense of humor. Thank them for their help and insights. Then thank them again. And again. And again and again!

- Reassure them often that they're special to you. Be romantic and give them cards, gifts, hugs, and so on.

- Join them in their enjoyment of life, and give them space, too; Twos have a conflict with dependence versus independence.

- Appreciate their ideal of wanting the world to be right and beautiful.

- Keep in mind that Twos may get very close to someone and lead them to think they are their best friend but disappear when they feel too needed, engulfed, or suffocated, especially extroverted Twos.

- Talk with them about their favorite subject:

- Be gentle and tactful when you have a criticism and don't tell them they are being illogical or taking things too personally unless you do it very gently.

- Let them know you approve of or admire their appearance and their accomplishments. Some Twos want *everybody* to know you love them!

You can give Twos extra support in these ways:

- Take an interest in their life and their problems, and don't let them transfer the focus to yours.

- Ask them to tell you honestly how they feel and what they want rather than telling you what they think you want to hear.

- Encourage them to learn to accept help. Twos feel embarrassed to ask for anything.

- Encourage them to risk expressing their anger and engaging in conflict. Take care to discuss boundaries that are safe for both of you.

- Encourage them to follow their personal and creative pursuits.

Janet enjoys being alone with her creative projects.

THE

ACHIEVER

Early to bed, early to rise,
work like hell, and advertise.
—Laurence J. Peter

Threes are motivated by the need to be well regarded, successful, productive, and efficient.

Twos, Threes, and Fours constitute the heart center of the Enneagram. Threes try to be seen in a positive light and tend to focus more on their outer appearance than on the way they feel.

Threes at Their BEST Are	Threes at Their WORST Are
energetic	self-centered
efficient	pretentious
optimistic	vain
industrious	superficial
self-propelled	vindictive
practical	overly competitive
responsible	deceptive
empowering	defensive
competent	opportunistic

Personality Inventory

Check what applies to you.

- ☐ 1 I continually try to live up to my potential and to achieve recognition.
- ☐ 2 I have energy to burn. The more I do, the better I feel; the better I feel, the more I do.
- ☐ 3 I have confidence in my abilities.
- ☐ 4 I carry out my projects with purpose and passion.
- ☐ 5 I am self-directed and am always setting new goals for myself.
- ☐ 6 I focus on what can be done rather than on what might go wrong.
- ☐ 7 I'm a good salesperson; it is easy for me to influence, motivate, and persuade.
- ☐ 8 Sometimes I sacrifice perfection for efficiency.
- ☐ 9 I like it when people admire my youthfulness and vitality.
- ☐ 10 Work seems to be more important to me than it is to my partner and friends.
- ☐ 11 I tend to avoid heavy talk about feelings.
- ☐ 12 I like to point out to my friends the positive things I've been doing: who I've seen, what's going on at work or at school, my political activities, how my athletic training is going, and so on. Sometimes I do this in a subtle or indirect way.
- ☐ 13 I am very aware of how people respond to me.
- ☐ 14 I am outgoing.
- ☐ 15 I fear getting too close and may move on when a relationship starts to become too intimate.
- ☐ 16 I get along well in diverse groups of people.
- ☐ 17 I am efficient, organized, and able to do many tasks at once.
- ☐ 18 All I accomplish may look easy to others, but I work hard at it.
- ☐ 19 I sometimes have envious thoughts about people who are more successful than I am.
- ☐ 20 I normally try to avoid confrontation.

Which Subtype Applies to You?

You May Relate to One, Two, or All Three Subtypes

Within each type there are three subtypes, representing the three aspects of instinctual life: personal well-being (*self-preservation*), one-to-one relationships (*relational*), and community (*social*). These subtypes or instincts are largely expressed in unconscious ways as we go about life. For most of us, the importance of one or more subtypes is exaggerated, though, and this interferes with our growth.

Threes need to be seen as successful in order to feel worthwhile and loved. They do so in the following ways, depending on their subtype. As they develop, Threes will move beyond these limitations and find contentment in just being.

Self-Preservation Threes: "Security"

- Financial security is of the utmost importance to me.

- I need to keep physically fit and stay in good health.

- I continually learn new skills and keep up on the latest developments in my field in order achieve and hang onto my career goals.

- I'm a good team player; I try to get along and stay away from conflict.

- I rarely take time off; when I go on vacations, I often take my work along.

- To me success doesn't necessarily mean being a leader or the center of attention. The person I'm trying to compete with and please is me.

Threes of this subtype are usually less extroverted and less concerned about image than the other two subtypes are and may be difficult to recognize as Threes.

Relational Threes: "Masculinity and Femininity"

- I try to impress the opposite sex with my charisma, success, sexiness, and strength.

43

- I have mastered the art of looking attractive.

- I pay great attention to what others find appealing and dress accordingly.

- I alter my behavior however I need to in order to keep my partner attracted to me.

- I want to be envied for having a great relationship with an admirable or prestigious person.

- I will avoid pursuing someone if there's a high chance of failing.

- I fear that people may want to reject me when they really get to know me.

Threes of this subtype often resemble the relational subtype of their Six arrow.

Social Threes: "Prestige"

Nothing succeeds
like address.

    —Fran Lebowitz

- I am an energetic, efficient, and strong-minded leader. I motivate people to do a good job, find clever solutions to problems, and I keep my audience's attention.

- I am proud of my friendships with other successful and powerful people.

- The organizations I belong to provide me with good opportunities to further my success.

- I get along in groups that are very different from one another.

- The way I fit into such disparate groups is by changing my personality and attire to meet the situation.

- Credentials, titles, and degrees are important to me.

- Nothing would be worse than to be anonymous.

- As a thinking type, I tend to focus on the group's goals. As a feeling type, I try to maintain harmony among the members.

Wings

Wings are the types on each side of your number. The Two wing influences the Three to be especially people oriented. The Four wing may add a strong imagination or a sense of melancholy.

Threes with a strong Two wing tend to be gregarious, helpful, socially adept, tuned in to others, charming, manipulative, possessive, and flattering.

Threes with a strong Four wing tend to be creative, introspective, private, subdued, intellectually oriented, moody, arrogant, and pretentious.

Occasionally people present the persona of one of their wings—rather than their actual type—to the outside world.

Arrows

Your personality is also influenced by the two types that are connected to yours by lines, the *arrows* of Six and Nine.

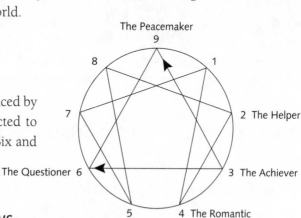

The Peacemaker
9
8   1
7
2 The Helper
The Questioner 6
3 The Achiever
5   4 The Romantic

How Wings and Arrows Influence Your Behavior in Relationships

We have a natural connection to our wings and arrows. They come into play without our knowing it: their positive aspects when we're feeling tranquil and integrated, and their unhealthy aspects during times of stress. When we want to change something about ourselves, we can try consciously to incorporate their favorable and avoid their negative traits. You may want to read the chapters on Twos, Fours, Sixes, and Nines to learn more about them.

As a Three, you are probably busy getting things done most of the time. Both your Two and Four wings can usher you into the worlds of feelings and meaningful relationships. You can become more helpful, affectionate, and sympathetic when you emulate your Two wing. Be aware of the Two's possessiveness and jealousy, though. Your Four wing can influence you to be more artistic, introspective, and sensitive. Some Four traits to avoid are being overly dramatic, snobbish, and aloof.

Your Six arrow can help you develop loyalty, commit more to your relationships, and work for causes you believe in. Be on the alert, however, for signs of hostility, in-

decisiveness, and dependence. If you want to slow down or work on being more receptive and attentive, go toward your Nine arrow. Your chance of a heart attack will decrease as winning becomes less important and taking time to relax becomes more important. Take caution, though, not to numb out, space out, or punish your loved ones passive-aggressively.

At their most developed, Threes are self-assured, well-rounded, optimistic, and accepting. They give others the recognition they have earned, and they work toward mutually beneficial solutions. Healthy Threes show the rest of us the joy that can come from skillfully carrying out meaningful goals.

Characteristics of Threes as Seen in Famous People and Roles

Speculations by the Authors

Articulate: Larry King, Bryant Gumbel, Oprah Winfrey, Diane Sawyer

Persuaders: Oral Roberts, Anthony Robbins, Werner Erhard of est

Optimists: Dick Clark, William Shatner as Captain Kirk on *Star Trek*

Athletically talented: Dorothy Hamill, Bruce Jenner, Steve Young

Wheeling and dealing: Michael Milken, Maurice on *Northern Exposure*

Masculine and feminine ideals: Sharon Stone, Wesley Snipes, Raquel Welch, Michelle Pfeiffer, Brooke Shields, Michael Landon, Kevin Costner, Cindy Crawford

Entertaining: Glen Campbell, John Davidson, Paula Abdul, Nora Ephron

Famous Pairs

Three and One:	Prince Philip and Queen Elizabeth II
Three and Two:	Jim and Tammy Faye Bakker
Three and Three:	Arnold Schwarzenegger and Maria Shriver
Three and Four:	F. Scott and Zelda Fitzgerald
Three and Five:	Sylvester Stallone and Talia Shire in *Rocky*
Three and Six:	Richard Dreyfuss and Bill Murray in *What About Bob?*
Three and Seven:	Demi Moore and Bruce Willis
Three and Eight:	Ivana and Donald Trump
Three and Nine:	Mary Tyler Moore and Donald Sutherland in *Ordinary People*

Achievers in Relationships

You never get a second chance to make a first impression.

—Head & Shoulders commercial

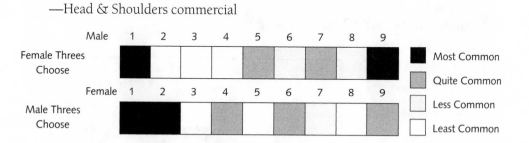

What Threes Say About Ones (Perfectionists)

I like Ones because they

- accomplish a great deal, just as I do

- present themselves well

- keep improving their skills

- carry out their ideals and their tasks with resolve

- are realistic, efficient, and dependable

I have trouble with Ones because they

- can be tense and make me feel uptight

- criticize me for not being as principled as they are

- withhold praise

- rarely forgive and forget a transgression

- self-righteously think their way of living is better than mine

What Threes Say About Twos (Helpers)

I like Twos because they

- anticipate my desires, support me, and treat me as important

- give me plenty of attention and affection

- are warm, understanding, and fun to be with

- make a good impression on others

- can socialize easily in any mixture of people

I have trouble with Twos because they

- get pouty when I don't do what they expect

- become overly emotional over practically nothing

- try to manipulate me into doing what they want

- demand too much attention from me

What Threes Say About Threes

I like Threes because we

- know how to get things done and are both highly productive

- understand each other's need to work hard

- both take pride in our appearance

- like to do physical activities together

- both enjoy socializing with interesting friends

I have trouble with Threes because we

- push ourselves too hard and get stressed and exhausted

- get distracted with work and don't give each other enough attention

- are both poor at expressing what we really feel

- withdraw when relationship problems come up

- can be too competitive

What Threes Say About Fours (Romantics)

I like Fours because they

- appreciate and encourage my talents and abilities

- have refined and elegant taste in clothes and decor

- are warm and put my clients, associates, and friends at ease

- are very entertaining and expressive, especially when extroverted

- help me become more individualistic and less interested in what others think of me; I like it that they are different from most other people

I have trouble with Fours because they

- unsettle me with their mood switches

- withdraw from me unpredictably

- can be a bottomless pit of emotional neediness

- criticize me for being superficial, for spending too much time working, and for not analyzing my feelings
- embarrass me when they act or dress too unconventionally

What Threes Say About Fives (Observers)

I like Fives because they

- are gentle with me
- take an interest in my projects and give me helpful feedback
- are quick-witted
- have a novel way of seeing things
- keep busy with their own projects and accept the time I devote to mine
- share their deep reserve of knowledge with me

I have trouble with Fives because they

- are often not practical enough; they can get abstract just when I want to get down to business
- withdraw, sulk, or get grumpy, although they seem to be devoted to the relationship
- may not be ambitious enough
- pay too little attention to their appearance
- are too private and unsociable

What Threes Say About Sixes (Questioners)

I like Sixes because they

- are conscientious and responsible

- usually have interesting minds and a good sense of humor

- value my work and accomplishments, but love me for who I am rather than for my image

- are warm and loyal, especially the feeling types; I know they are on my side and I don't worry that they'll run off with someone else

I have trouble with Sixes because they

- blame their problems on others instead of taking responsibility for them

- take the tiniest slight as total rejection, especially the feeling-type Sixes

- insult people and have a superior air, especially the thinking-type Sixes

- never entertain the possibility that things might turn out all right; they drive me crazy with their pessimism and *anxiety*

51

What Threes Say About Sevens (Adventurers)

I like Sevens because they

- are positive, lively, and cheerful

- are interested in and good at doing many things; they have plenty to keep them busy when I'm immersed in my work

- are cheerful, positive, and lively; they're always thinking up exciting things for us to do

- have as much energy as I do and keep up with me

- are full of fun surprises

I have trouble with Sevens because they

- are not accountable

- are usually not orderly enough

- change their minds too often

- get sidetracked easily and drop their responsibilities in my lap

- can be blunt or rude and put me down or make thoughtless comments

- seem to feel superior to me

What Threes Say About Eights (Asserters)

I like Eights because they

- are usually self-confident, capable, and successful

- put enormous energy into whatever they do

- encourage me to be honest and direct

- set a good example by not being concerned about what people think of them

- are loyal, giving, and loving

I have trouble with Eights because they

- are quick to fault me for being superficial

- are possessive, overbearing, and brooding

- sometimes use shocking, abrasive, or off-color language

- don't always treat people well

- are likely to blow up at me or someone else

What Threes Say About Nines (Peacemakers)

I like Nines because they

- understand me in a fundamental way

- have a relaxing and calming influence on me; I can space out with them and not feel guilty

- listen to me and support me

- go along with me in doing the things I enjoy

- are not judgmental

- admire my drive and productivity

I have trouble with Nines because they

- don't match my fast pace

- procrastinate when there are things to get done

- don't let me know what they want, even with small things such as choosing a movie or a restaurant

- constantly question whether what they want to do is really what they want to do

---

Things Threes Would Never Dream of Doing . . .

☞ walking meditatively and slowly up the steps instead of running up three at a time

☞ getting an invitation to a prestigious event and not feeling smug that their rivals weren't invited

☞ failing to mention the prestigious university they graduated from

☞ getting excited about getting older

☞ not buffing up for their high school reunion

☞ meeting their current love's ex and not comparing physiques

☞ encouraging their costar to make the speech at the Emmy awards when only one of them is allowed on stage

☞ allowing more than a fifteen-minute cry over the breakup of their five-year relationship

How to Get Along with Threes

- Acknowledge their achievements and success.

- Understand and appreciate that an important way they give to a relationship is through their effort and diligence.

- Realize that they can be ill at ease when not being productive. Leave them alone when they are busy, and add to your own interests if necessary.

- Give them honest, objective feedback, being very sensitive to their feelings.

- Be aware that they can easily feel judged as being superficial.

- Avoid bringing up their past mistakes, focusing on negatives, and talking excessively about the relationship.

- Work together on common goals. Threes relate well through productive activity.

- Admire their confidence, optimism, efficiency, and boundless energy.

You can give Threes extra support in these ways:

- Though Threes are usually assertive in their professional life, they can use encouragement to be direct and ask for what they want in their personal life.

- Support them in developing good friendships.

- Encourage them to slow down and relax. Threes are always in a hurry.

55

- Encourage them to work for causes they believe in.

- Encourage them to nurture their inner lives.

- Take an interest in their feelings.

Jacques is learning to feel safe about opening his heart and showing his fears, doubts, and longings.

THE

ROMANTIC

I feel so bad since you've gone. It's almost like having you here.

—Anonymous

Fours are motivated by the need to understand their feelings, to search for what is missing and for what life means, and to avoid being ordinary. They are "romantic" in the sense of having an imaginative or artistic personality.

Twos, Threes, and Fours constitute the heart center of the Enneagram. Fours need to express their feelings and to be seen as special. Since they compare reality with what could be, they find fault with who they are and what they have.

unavailable

distant

Fours at Their BEST Are	Fours at Their WORST Are
individualistic	temperamental
perceptive	withdrawn
expressive	self-absorbed
creative	envious
warm	emotionally needy
supportive	easily hurt
refined	snobbish
compassionate	depressed
gentle	critical
witty	self-indulgent

Personality Inventory

Check what applies to you.

☐ 1 People are attracted to me for my creativity, warmth, and depth of feelings.

☐ 2 I am in touch with the sorrowful and tragic aspects of life.

☐ 3 Being misunderstood is especially painful to me.

☐ 4 I long, or have longed, for the perfect soul mate to come along.

☐ 5 I am, or have been, attracted to unattainable, unavailable, or inappropriate people.

☐ 6 I am supportive and compassionate, especially when someone is in a crisis.

☐ 7 Life seems terribly mundane and boring at times.

☐ 8 I easily soak up others' pain.

☐ 9 I sometimes feel melancholy; I pity myself or long for what others have that I do not have.

☐ 10 I am drawn to what is intense and out of the ordinary.

☐ 11 I have many dreams and ideals, but sometimes I have a hard time actualizing them.

☐ 12 I feel things more deeply than the average person and suspect those who always act happy.

☐ 13 I have a rich and active imagination and like to put things together in new ways.

☐ 14 I have a flair for clothes and enjoy looking a bit offbeat.

☐ 15 I often feel self-conscious.

☐ 16 I believe I am flawed at a deep level.

☐ 17 It has been difficult to find a relationship in which I really feel loved.

☐ 18 Sometimes my love interest or partner seems more attractive to me when he or she is away.

☐ 19 I try to hold my feelings back so they won't scare people off.

☐ 20 I have been or have felt abandoned.

Which Subtype Applies to You?

You May Relate to One, Two, or All Three Subtypes

Within each type there are three subtypes, representing the three aspects of instinctual life: personal well-being (*self-preservation*), one-to-one relationships (*relational*), and community (*social*). These subtypes or instincts are largely expressed in unconscious ways as we go about life. For most of us, the importance of one or more subtypes is exaggerated, though, and this interferes with our growth.

Fours cope with, and divert attention from, their need to be special and their feelings of loss in the following ways, depending on their subtype. As they develop, Fours will move beyond these limitations, learn to live in the reality of the present, and feel truly deserving of love.

Self-Preservation Fours: "Dauntless"

- I crave intensity and stimulation in order to feel alive and avoid the dullness and meaningless of a mundane existence.

- I am attracted to being close to birth, death, catastrophe, and serious illness.

- I have plunged into dangerous situations, for example, taking physical risks, breaking laws or rules, taking chances with my money, engaging in promiscuity, or entering into unhealthy relationships.

- I can be determined and persevering in pulling myself and others through crises.

- I rebel strenuously when people attack my ideals, tell me what to do, or try to change me. I may hurl sarcastic remarks or fly into a rage.

- I focus intently on my creative work or causes.

- I can see myself excluding everything else that is going on around me and ignoring the necessities of day-to-day survival while I pursue my goal.

- I like to point out angles that others have not thought of.

- I take great offense when people assume they know what I think and how I feel.

Relational Fours: "Competition and Envy"

- I envy people who seem happier, more fulfilled, or more interesting than I am, particularly those whose assets are similar to mine.

- When having problems in a relationship, I am more likely to become depressed than angry.

- I want my partner to experience our relationship as unique and intense.

- I'm attracted to what is distant and unattainable.

- I long, or have longed, for a soul mate or Prince or Princess Charming to come along and rescue me from an ordinary life.

- I frequently get my partner to leave, then try to win him or her back. This push and pull creates drama and pain, keeps renewing the distance I want, and gives me the feeling that I am in control.

- Getting close frightens me because my loved one might discover that I don't measure up to the ideal.

- I sometimes feel I'm not special enough to be truly loved.

Social Fours: "Shame"

One may have a blazing hearth in one's soul,
and yet no one ever comes to sit by it.

—Vincent van Gogh

Shame, as we use it here, means embarrassment, humiliation, and lack of self-respect.

- I feel ashamed of not measuring up to my vision of the ideal: not being bright or creative enough, not contributing to humanity, or not having a fulfilling relationship.

- I die over each mistake or faux pas I make.

- I often feel inadequate socially and either try to pour on charm and confidence or blend into the woodwork.

- I'm always analyzing myself: Did I make myself understood? Did I sound stupid? Was I too aggressive? Was I too conciliatory?

- I have dreams of achieving tremendous status and recognition in order to get revenge on those who have put me down or laughed at me.

- I am very sensitive to being shamed or slighted. It devastates me to be excluded from a gathering or event that acquaintances or friends are attending.

- Sometimes I say things against myself to try to deflect envy.

- I feel less awkward when I fill a definite position in the group by demonstrating that I'm an authority on something or by making a strong statement about who I am by the way I dress.

Wings

Wings are the types on each side of your number. Fours with more developed Three wings are usually more lively. The Five wing is responsible for a more contemplative or intellectual personality.

Fours with a strong Three wing tend to be energetic, active, outgoing, competitive, ambitious, attention seeking, and elitist.

Fours with a strong Five wing tend to be objective, quiet, unconventional, original, enigmatic, alienated, pessimistic, analytical, and withdrawn.

Occasionally people present the persona of one of their wings—rather than their actual type—to the outside world.

Arrows

Your personality is also influenced by the types that are connected to yours by lines, the *arrows* of One and Two.

9

8   1 The Perfectionist

7   2 The Helper

6   3 The Achiever

The Observer 5   4 The Romantic

How Wings and Arrows Influence
Your Behavior in Relationships

We have a natural connection to our wings and arrows. They come into play without our knowing it: their positive aspects when we're feeling tranquil and integrated, and their unhealthy aspects during times of stress. When we want to change something about ourselves, we can try consciously to incorporate their favorable and avoid their negative traits. You may want to read the chapters on Threes, Fives, Ones, and Twos to learn more about your wings and arrows.

There is quite a contrast between a Four with a dominant Three wing, and a Four with a dominant Five wing.

If you lean toward your Three wing, you are probably extroverted and sociable, upbeat, image conscious, and possibly flamboyant. You can summon up energy and productivity through this wing. Keep in check the urge to impress others, and don't lose focus on your creativity.

If you lean toward your Five wing, you have traits in common with the head center as well as your heart center. Since Fives are generally introverted, you are likely to be serious, intellectual, and reserved. If your emotional energy feels overwhelming, steer yourself toward this more objective wing. Watch out for the tendency to be negative or reclusive, however.

Your practical One arrow can be used to bring out your ability to organize, to be objective, and to act on your ideals. It can influence you to become less self-indulgent and less controlled by your feelings. Be aware of the tendency to be self-critical, guilt ridden, or demanding.

Your Two arrow can help you to be more accommodating, less self-absorbed, and to act on your ideal of service to others. Watch this arrow's influence on you to become codependent or manipulative. Sometimes Fours with a strong Two arrow try to get someone else to prove their worth, or they become ill to get their partner's attention.

Healthy Fours are gentle and bond well. They are appreciated for their warmth, passion, and wit and for their ability to perceive what is beautiful in life.

Characteristics of Fours as Seen in Famous People and Roles

Speculations by the Authors

Very dramatic: Marlon Brando, Sarah Bernhardt, Isadora Duncan, Judy Garland, John Malkovich

Soul-searching: Alan Watts, Fyodor Dostoevsky, Chris on *Northern Exposure*

Talented and creative: Joni Mitchell, James Taylor, Judy Collins, Tennessee Williams, John Keats, Edna St. Vincent Millay, Anthony Hopkins, Winona Ryder, Edgar Allen Poe, Liam Neeson, Rudolf Nureyev, Martha Graham

Envious: Snow White's stepmother, Hansel and Gretel's stepmother

Self-absorbed: Kelsey Grammer on *Cheers* and *Frasier,* Françoise Sagan

Dying over love: Madame Bovary, Anna Karenina

Humorous and biting: Dick Cavett, Dorothy Parker, Oscar Wilde

*Melancholy men are of
all others the most witty.*
  —Aristotle

Sensitive: Gustave Flaubert, Charles-Pierre Baudelaire, Marcel Proust, James Dean, Lord Byron, Claude Debussy, Franz Schubert

Depressed: Kurt Cobain, Sylvia Plath, Virginia Woolf, Edvard Munch, Vincent van Gogh, Frida Kahlo

Famous Pairs

Four and One: Charlie Brown and Lucy

Four and Two: Montgomery Clift and Elizabeth Taylor in *A Place in the Sun*

Four and Three: Ted Dobson and Kathy Hurley, Enneagram authors

Four and Four: Liv Ullman and Ingmar Bergman

Four and Five: Jane and Paul Bowles

Four and Six: Ophelia and Hamlet

Four and Seven: Jackie and John F. Kennedy

Four and Eight: Jackie Kennedy and Aristotle Onassis

Four and Nine: Paul Simon and Art Garfunkel

Romantics in Relationships

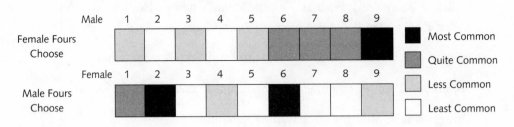

	Male	1	2	3	4	5	6	7	8	9
Female Fours Choose										

	Female	1	2	3	4	5	6	7	8	9
Male Fours Choose										

- ■ Most Common
- ▦ Quite Common
- ▨ Less Common
- □ Least Common

What Fours Say About Ones (Perfectionists)

I like Ones because they

- follow through on their promises and commitments

- appreciate my high ideals, and I appreciate theirs

- influence me to be practical and to handle the details of my life in an organized and efficient way

- want to better themselves, so they are usually willing to accompany me to the cultural events I like to attend

- have a good sense of humor and can be very playful, especially with the help of their Seven (Adventurer) arrow

I have trouble with Ones because they

- bring out my shame and lack of self-esteem by giving me critical looks

- are self-righteous and try to get me to do everything their way

- can be poor at expressing their feelings and judgmental about mine

- see things in terms of black and white

What Fours Say About Twos (Helpers)

I like Twos because they

- spend plenty of time with me, listen to my problems, and understand my feelings

- praise my creativity and my good taste

- enliven me with their enthusiasm and joie de vivre

- give me the feeling that I am truly loved

I have trouble with Twos because they

- are too positive, nice, and smiley

- complain that I am stuck in always processing my feelings

- judge me for my style and for feeling melancholy

- give me advice when I just want to be understood

What Fours Say About Threes (Achievers)

I like Threes because they

- are often attractive and charming

- make me feel taken care of

- seem to know what they want

- encourage me to get things done and to engage in my creative activities

- have an optimistic and enthusiastic attitude, which balances my dark moods

- become involved in causes that benefit the world, especially healthy Threes

I have trouble with Threes because they

- are out of touch with the dark side of life

- seem to be judging me but don't express it directly

- will do almost anything to be accepted, including denying all their defects

- try to come up with a quick fix when I'm in pain or depressed

- are too tied to convention and the work ethic
- slip out of things they've agreed to do with me because they're too busy

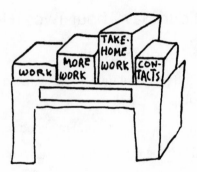

What Fours Say About Fours

I like Fours because we

- share in our depth of feelings and interest in aesthetics
- empathize with each other when melancholy or depressed
- are both truly involved in our relationship
- can be extremely funny together
- can discuss subjects that most people aren't interested in, such as the intuitive and creative process

I have trouble with Fours because we

- often have different styles of being Fours; for instance, I may be introverted and quiet and offended by Romantics who are showy and theatrical
- both can become depressed and nonfunctional for days at a time
- can get nasty and blaming
- become resentful when the other fails to live up to our expectations of the perfect partner; this shows the connection to our One arrow

What Fours Say About Fives (Observers)

I like Fives because they

- are soft-spoken, gentle, and have a caring presence about them
- have a stabilizing effect on our relationship
- are inquisitive and thoughtful and give me meaningful insights
- have many interests in common with me: ideas, art, music, nature, and traveling

- are unconventional, as I am

- have the capacity, which I am trying to develop, to detach and to be objective

I have trouble with Fives because they

- have an arsenal of clever ways to distance themselves from me and activate my feelings of abandonment

- seem ambivalent about whether they want to be in a relationship

- can be indifferent about their appearance

- seem cold and unfeeling at times yet judge me for being too emotional

What Fours Say About Sixes (Questioners)

I like Sixes because they

- show their love through the efforts they make to understand me

- have sharp minds and ironic wit

- have a rebellious side, as I do, and can be mysterious and electrifying

- fear being abandoned or misunderstood, as I do, and try to help me feel safe

I have trouble with Sixes because they

- often challenge what I say, which leads to stormy arguments

- make me nervous by worrying, fretting, and agonizing over decisions

- have a mean streak and can be mistrustful, blaming, and cynical

- can erode my confidence by questioning my abilities

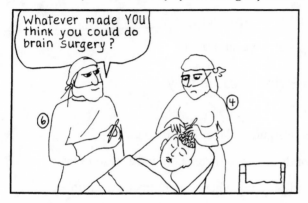

What Fours Say About Sevens (Adventurers)

I like Sevens because they

- have quick, playful, and curious minds

- think up unique things for us to do

- supply the energy and intensity I crave

- are irreverent and antiauthoritarian, as I am

I have trouble with Sevens because they

- seem to embody the best of all worlds when I first meet them but disappoint me later by displaying a lack of emotional depth

- are attracted to me because I am unique, interesting, and deep and later complain that I need to lighten up

- either run out of the room or joke and tease when I am serious or depressed

- don't like negativity; as a result, I tend to hold back my feelings

What Fours Say About Eights (Asserters)

I like Eights because they

- appreciate my ability to engage with them intensely

- can use their exuberance to shock me out of the doldrums

- remain solid when I become depressed or emotional

- encourage me to put my creative work out into the world

- are outrageous, unpretentious, and direct

I have trouble with Eights because they

- have gauche manners

- sometimes can goad me and make cruel remarks

- put too many demands on me and come on like a steamroller

- can get disgusted and rejecting when I am in my own world

What Fours Say About Nines (Peacemakers)

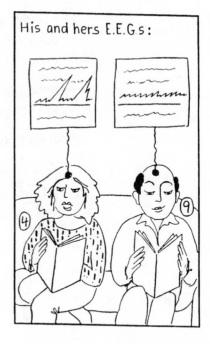

His and hers E.E.G.s:

I like Nines because they

- are nonjudgmental

- treat me gently

- have a spiritual and empathic sense about them

- like to participate in what I do and connect with me intimately

- do not try to change or threaten me

- are usually able to stay with what I am expressing even if they don't completely understand it

I have trouble with Nines because they

- can be too conciliatory and smooth everything over

- don't challenge me enough

- are too unclear when trying to communicate their feelings, desires, or other information

- vanish into their world of habits and routines and leave me feeling abandoned

---

Things Fours Would Never Dream of Doing . . .

- ☞ describing their twenty-page journal entry to their partner in two minutes

- ☞ finding the decor of the room offensive—yet ignoring it

- ☞ overhearing spiteful accusations and gossip about themselves, laughing it off lightly, and not dropping a bit in their self-esteem level

- ☞ receiving a terrible review of their performance by the only critic they respect and not getting depressed

☞ not giving one moment's thought to finding a unique outfit to wear on their date with the person of their dreams

☞ deciding that thirty minutes was more than enough time to lament over their ended relationship

☞ feeling totally proud of their mundane job

☞ talking about only the happy events in their childhood, and even if they could think of only one, repeating that one over and over

How to Get Along with Fours

- Appreciate their creativity, perception, and depth of feeling.

- Don't push them to socialize, especially the introverted Fours.

- Acknowledge their feelings and changing moods, and be honest about how these affect you.

- Encourage them to collect more information when they feel offended to see if there was a misunderstanding.

- Show your love frequently.

- Keep in mind that criticism can activate their feelings of shame.

- But remember, it is not good for either of you to be controlled by their moods or fragility.

- Be honest in a caring way about how it affects you when they are unrealistic, overly sensitive, or have their head in the clouds.

- Don't offer easy solutions for their pain.

- Try to lighten them up only when they really want you to.

- Be understanding about their need to process and express their feelings.

There is something pleasurable in calm remembrance of a past sorrow.
—Cicero

You can give Fours extra support in these ways:

- Help them feel safe about expressing their intense feelings and anger.

- Try to be strong and stay centered when they do their push-pull game. Be honest about how you feel about this, however, and seek counseling if necessary.

- Understand their need for independence and autonomy.

- Encourage them to take pleasure in the present, to be creative (through writing, art, music, dance, etc.), and to put their work out in the world.

- Encourage them to find a meaningful career where they can use their compassion.

THE

OBSERVER

Why one has to have a body, I don't know.
A necessary appendage to the head, I suppose.

—Paul Bowles

Fives are motivated by the need to know and understand, to be self-sufficient, and to avoid feeling engulfed or invaded.

Fives, Sixes, and Sevens constitute the head center of the Enneagram. Fives are fearful, hypersensitive to people, accumulate information, and like being alone with their own thoughts or interests.

Fives at Their BEST Are	Fives at Their WORST Are
objective	contentious
focused	arrogant
wise	stingy
kind	critical of others
open-minded	negative
perceptive	withdrawn
trustworthy	stubborn
calm	judgmental
curious	withholding
insightful	alienated

Personality Inventory

Check what applies to you.

- ☐ 1 I don't like invasive or overly emotional people, especially those who are angry or aggressive.
- ☐ 2 I tend to be self-reliant and keep my problems to myself.
- ☐ 3 Routines such as eating, sleeping, or changing my clothes become relatively unimportant when I'm reading or concentrating on one of my projects.
- ☐ 4 I often feel shy and uncomfortable around people.
- ☐ 5 I feel more at ease expressing my thoughts than my feelings.
- ☐ 6 I enjoy spending a lot of my time alone.
- ☐ 7 I generally wait for people to approach me instead of approaching them.
- ☐ 8 Occasionally I feel righteous enough to become angry.
- ☐ 9 I am better able to experience how I feel about something afterward, when I am alone.
- ☐ 10 I don't like social functions: parties and small talk don't appeal to me except with family and people I know well.
- ☐ 11 I don't like to be asked broad, general questions about myself.
- ☐ 12 I like being appreciated for my knowledge.
- ☐ 13 I try not to be involved in confrontations.
- ☐ 14 I don't usually want people to know how I feel or what I'm thinking unless I tell them.
- ☐ 15 When others try to regulate my life, I feel frantic and angry.
- ☐ 16 I can be cynical and argumentative.
- ☐ 17 I usually work things out in my mind before I talk about them; I often hesitate while I try to order my thoughts and may not speak at all if I can't perfect what I want to say.
- ☐ 18 At times I wish I had better social skills.
- ☐ 19 People sometimes find it difficult to follow my train of thought.
- ☐ 20 I have little interest in most social conventions.

Which Subtype Applies to You?

You May Relate to One, Two, or All Three Subtypes

Within each type there are three subtypes, representing the three aspects of instinctual life: personal well-being (*self-preservation*), one-to-one relationships (*relational*), and community (*social*). These subtypes or instincts are largely expressed in unconscious ways as we go about life. For most of us, the importance of one or more subtypes is exaggerated, though, and this interferes with our growth.

Fives cope with their anxiety in the following ways, depending on their subtype. As they move beyond these limitations, they will feel less smothered and controlled and interact more easily.

Self-Preservation Fives: "My Home Is My Castle"

I never found the companion that
was so companionable as solitude.

 —Henry David Thoreau

- I need to live in a private place where I can concentrate; I want no expectations, intrusions, demands, questions, coercion, or noise.

- I try to keep my life simple.

- The more time I spend with people, the more drained I become.

- It would bog me down to have a lot of belongings; I need easy access to books and other information though.

- I have a tendency to save; I protect both my time and my money.

- I am self-reliant; it rarely occurs to me to seek help or advice.

- I dislike owing or being owed anything.

Some of the most introverted of all the nine types are of this subtype.

Relational Fives: "Confidences"

- My close relationships often involve sharing secrets such as inside information with a colleague, a piece of forbidden knowledge about someone, or a made-up language with a friend or lover.

- Keeping things to myself can give me a feeling of excitement and power; I have taken revenge by *not* telling something that I knew people wanted to know.

- I don't want my partner to discuss our relationship or private business without consulting me first.

- I like to have interesting conversations, although I rarely initiate them with people I don't know; as a thinking type, I tend to discuss logistics, scientific matters, or mechanics; as a feeling type, I am more likely to discuss literature, the arts, or psychology.

- I especially value the people I know who respect my boundaries.

- I know I look aloof, but I'm often very involved with what is going on as an observer. I find this more comfortable than having to be a part of the action, where I might feel inadequate or put on the spot.

- Expressing my feelings sensually is very important to me, because this gets me out of my head and into my body.

- When I'm alone with my feelings, they seem quite clear; but when I try to express them to my partner and close friends, I can't find the right words.

Social Fives: "Recognition and Hierarchy"

- I prefer to work in a flexible, unstructured way and to set my own goals.

- I like either to be self-employed or to have a safe nook in the hierarchy of a university or company where I can be relatively autonomous.

- Rules and regulations often get in my way.

- When I do high-quality work, I like praise from people who matter to me, but I don't usually ask for it.

- Either I attend meetings in order to pick up knowledge and meet interesting people, or I avoid groups and organizations altogether.

- As an extrovert, I like overt attention for my ideas and contributions. As an introvert, I am usually satisfied by having my work known and my name respected but am embarrassed by showy accolades.

- I love to dig out information and find out what the experts in my field, and in other fields, have to say.

Social Fives usually appear more extroverted than other Fives.

Wings

Wings are the types on each side of your number. Fives with a strong Four wing tend to be relatively people-oriented. Fives with a strong Six wing vary a lot but tend to have scientific or intellectual interests.

Fives with a strong Four wing tend to be artistic, imaginative, self-absorbed, personal, sensitive to feelings, moody, melancholy, and interested in aesthetics.

Fives with a strong Six wing tend to be logical, analytical, intellectual, hardworking, anxious, afraid of intimacy, socially awkward, and skeptical.

Occasionally people present the persona of one of their wings—rather than their actual type—to the outside world.

Arrows

Your personality is also influenced by the two types that are connected to yours by lines, the *arrows* of Seven and Eight.

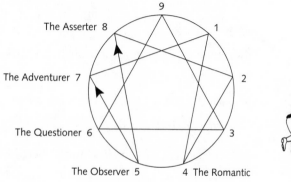

How Wings and Arrows Influence Your Behavior in Relationships

We have a natural connection to our wings and arrows. They often come into play without our knowing it: their positive aspects when we're feeling tranquil and integrated, and their unhealthy aspects during times of stress. When we want to change something about ourselves, we can try consciously to incorporate their favorable and to avoid their negative traits. You may want to read the chapters on Fours, Sixes, Sevens, and Eights to learn more about them.

Fives are in the head center and can feel somewhat backward as far as people and relationships go. Your Four wing can provide empathy, warmth, and insight. Watch out that you don't become self-absorbed or hypersensitive, however. Emulate your Six wing for developing loyalty, idealism, and intellectual playfulness. But be aware of being argumentative, paranoid, or afraid of intimacy.

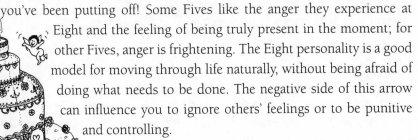

Your Eight arrow is a source of energy and action. It can give you the initiative you need to speak up and to make that phone call for a date or appointment that you've been putting off! Some Fives like the anger they experience at Eight and the feeling of being truly present in the moment; for other Fives, anger is frightening. The Eight personality is a good model for moving through life naturally, without being afraid of doing what needs to be done. The negative side of this arrow can influence you to ignore others' feelings or to be punitive and controlling.

Most Fives want to be less self-conscious and less inhibited. Your Seven arrow is a fine model for this. You can also become more enthusiastic, irresistibly lovable, witty, and whimsical when you bring out your Seven arrow. Be aware of becoming distracted easily or hurting relationships by spending too much time with your projects.

At their most developed, Fives have interesting, sometimes brilliant minds, are kind, perceptive, and trustworthy, and have a deep sense of integrity.

Characteristics of Fives as Seen in Famous People and Roles

Speculations by the Authors

Scientific: Stephen Hawking, Albert Einstein, Oliver Sacks, Linus Pauling, Thomas Edison, Sam Neill in *Jurassic Park*

Philosophical: Immanuel Kant, Simone Weil, Georg W. F. Hegel, René Descartes, Thomas Hobbes, David Hume, John Stuart Mill, Albert Camus

Watching: James Spader in *sex, lies, and videotape*

Soft-spoken: Arthur Ashe

Political: Paul Tsongas, Eugene McCarthy, Adlai Stevenson

I have noticed that nothing I
never said ever did me any harm.
> —Calvin "Silent Cal" Coolidge

Eccentric: Howard Hughes, J. Paul Getty, Bobby Fischer

Reclusive: Daniel Day-Lewis, Greta Garbo, cartoonist R. Crumb

Quietly strong: Max von Sydow, Clint Eastwood, Charles Bronson

Whimsical: David Byrne of the Talking Heads

Abstract: Emily Dickinson, James Joyce, Marianne Moore

Innovative: Stanley Kubrick, Henri Matisse, Georgia O'Keeffe, Paul Cézanne, Franz Kafka, Bill Gates of Microsoft

Famous Pairs

Five and One: Hume Cronyn and Jessica Tandy

Five and Two: Daniel Day-Lewis and Isabelle Adjani

Five and Three: Eliot and Bev in *Dead Ringers*

Five and Four: Frédéric Chopin and George Sand

Five and Five: Lenin and Marx

Five and Six: Paul Newman and Robert Redford in *The Sting*

Five and Seven: Robert MacNeil and Jim Lehrer of PBS

Five and Eight: Richard Burton and Elizabeth Taylor in *Who's Afraid of Virginia Woolf?*

Five and Nine: Marie and Pierre Curie

Observers in Relationships

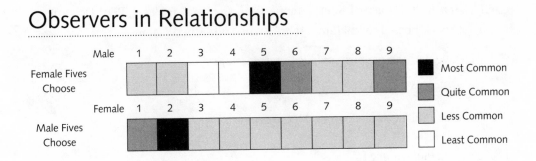

What Fives Say About Ones (Perfectionists)

Male	1	2	3	4	5	6	7	8	9

Female Fives Choose

| Female | 1 | 2 | 3 | 4 | 5 | 6 | 7 | 8 | 9 |

Male Fives Choose

Most Common
Quite Common
Less Common
Least Common

What Fives Say About Ones (Perfectionists)

I like Ones because they

- are independent, objective, and retain control of their emotions
- think things through carefully, study up, and then take sensible action
- are cautious and reasonable in financial and other matters
- take control of household and social details that I find boring
- do what they say they're going to do

I have trouble with Ones because they

- are overly anxious
- can be unbending and judgmental
- tell me what to do and when to do it; I feel like bolting when I'm told I *must* do something
- think I am being critical when I'm just being my naturally quiet self
- want to do what they think we *should* do instead of what we are *interested* in doing

What Fives Say About Twos (Helpers)

I like Twos because they

- treat me with kindness, generosity, and sensitivity
- help me feel appreciated and liked
- are at ease with people, which takes the burden off me when we socialize

- have a good sense of humor and appreciate my wit

- admire my calmness and steadiness

- express their feelings well and inspire me to express mine

I have trouble with Twos because they

- want to socialize more than I do

- are not willing to challenge me

- get too emotional and embarrass me by showing off

- constantly seek approval

- don't say what it is they want

- intrude on me when I'm busy

What Fives Say About Threes (Achievers)

I like Threes because they

- are busy with their own activities and usually not too demanding of me

- have a lot of drive and energy

- seem to know what they want

- keep well informed and express their thoughts cogently

- are competent and keep things running smoothly

I have trouble with Threes because they

- have a different value system from me, which includes being too concerned with social norms and with what people think of them

- live at a frantic pace and spend too much time away from home

- pretend they know more than they do and brag about their accomplishments

- take themselves too seriously

What Fives Say About Fours (Romantics)

I like Fours because they

- have rich and interesting inner lives

- enjoy spending time alone

- are often eccentric and accept my nonconforming ways

- can engage with me in analytical and challenging discussions

- have a well-developed aesthetic sense

- challenge me to express my feelings

I have trouble with Fours because they

- put on airs

- become hurt so easily that I must always walk on eggs

- demand attention from me when I want to be alone, especially extroverted Fours

- try to involve me in processing their feelings; I don't like being engulfed by their dismal murkiness

- confuse me and deplete me with their mood swings

- can be so critical that it gets in the way of the intimacy they are looking for

What Fives Say About Fives

I like Fives because we

- are both understated and accept being together in a quiet way; neither of us feels compelled to entertain

- are both responsible and ethical
- find each other's unusual viewpoints and perceptions intriguing
- understand each other with little effort
- each have well thought-out ideas and philosophies that make for interesting discussions
- give each other room

I have trouble with Fives because we

- both make biting verbal attacks and ignore each other
- get caught up in our own worlds and sometimes have difficulty coming together
- reinforce each other's cautiousness and anxiety
- fail to be supportive at times
- represent to each other some of the qualities we don't want to accept in ourselves (our shadow issues)

What Fives Say About Sixes (Questioners)

I like Sixes because they

- are often warm and nonjudgmental
- are in the same head center as I am and are mentally quick, curious, and knowledgeable
- usually have a good sense of humor
- usually respect my need to be alone
- understand my fears
- are loyal and trustworthy and make me feel secure *most of the time*

I have trouble with Sixes because they

- sap my energy by being overly anxious and paranoid; their demands for reassurance drive me nuts

- are unpredictable; I often can't tell whether they want to be close or distant from me

- see my detachment as a threat

- can be too dependent and too domineering, even at the same time

- are too quick to judge and blame

What Fives Say About Sevens (Adventurers)

I like Sevens because they

- are jovial, lively, carefree, and bring out my silliness

- share my attitude that nothing is sacred, especially the thinking-type Sevens

HIS and HERS Castles

- are independent yet can become interested in whatever I am working on or thinking about

- are at home in social situations

- generate new and fascinating activities and ideas

I have trouble with Sevens because they

- need to learn how to focus and explore in depth; they can lose interest in our projects just when I'm getting started

- stay away from home too much and are too busy and energetic when they're here

- are "on" all the time, demanding too much attention from me

- pressure me to socialize

- can be unreliable, unpunctual, and unpredictable

What Fives Say About Eights (Asserters)

I like Eights because they

- value self-reliance and independence

- distrust authority, as I do

- have no problem defending their actions and ideas or speaking up for the underdog

- believe in their ability to produce change

- react quickly and spontaneously (which I wish would rub off on me!)

- can be exhilarating to lock horns with when their arguing is honest and fair and doesn't wipe me out

I have trouble with Eights because they

- are too heavy-handed; they use sledgehammers when feathers would do

- challenge everything I say and start too many arguments

- often use offensive language or talk too loudly

- think it's up to them to judge all transgressions

- can be negative and alienated, as I can be, which hurts the relationship

What Fives Say About Nines (Peacemakers)

I like Nines because they

- enjoy exploring many areas of knowledge

- are refreshingly modest, down-to-earth, and unaffected

- are nonjudgmental, tolerant, and kind

- don't usually pressure me to do things I don't want to do

- can enjoy physical contact and appreciate nonverbal communication

- appreciate what I have to offer in terms of analysis and advice

I have trouble with Nines because they

- tune me out or ramble without getting to the point and then feel abandoned when I detach

- automatically agree with me instead of analyzing what I've said and coming to their own conclusion

- show their anger in passive-aggressive ways instead of directly

- might not mind spending every minute with me

Things Fives Would Never Dream of Doing . . .

☞ inviting some relatives they've never met to join them on their vacation

☞ applying for the position of social director on Partyship Cruise Lines

☞ spending eight hours at the mall trying on clothes

☞ not seething when their colleague wins the Nobel Prize for chemistry even though the Five did most of the work

☞ crying hysterically in front of the whole department when the chair informs them they won't get to teach their favorite class, "Obscure Minutiae of Thermodynamic Theory"

☞ selling underwear or plastic kitchen containers at giggly parties

☞ not saying or thinking "I know" for a week

☞ holding back their answers to trivia games so the other players won't feel inferior

☞ deciding that reading ten more books on their favorite subject would be a total waste of time

How to Get Along with Fives

• Appreciate their objectivity, intellect, and wit.

• Speak straightforwardly and briefly.

• Let them know you value the wisdom of their counsel and advice, if you do.

• Take special notice when they give without being asked. For instance, a Five may take pleasure in showing his or her feelings by making improvements around the house.

• Tell them what you want or need in a matter-of-fact, nondemanding way.

• Respect their need for privacy while they work on their ideas or projects. Develop your own friends, interests, and hobbies rather than depending on them for all your companionship.

- Never embarrass them or put them on the spot.

- Help maintain a harmonious household, free of surprises.

- If you want to do something new, give them plenty of time to get used to the idea.

- Don't pressure them to socialize.

- Try to be objective when working out problems. Strong emotional displays are usually counterproductive.

- Pinpoint problems you're having with them and set aside specific, limited times to discuss them.

- Engage with them in interesting and stimulating conversation, but avoid filling the gaps with chatter.

In Maine we have a saying
that there's no point in speaking
unless you can improve on silence.

    —Edmund Muskie

- Don't try to force them to act more enthusiastic than they feel or to conform to your preconceived image of them.

THE

QUESTIONER

I don't like being afraid. It scares me.

—Margaret "Hot Lips" Houlihan, *M.A.S.H.*

Sixes are motivated by the need for security. Phobic Sixes show their fear and seek approval, while counterphobic Sixes are daring or confrontational and hide their fear. Phobic and counterphobic traits often appear in the same person.

Fives, Sixes, and Sevens constitute the head center of the Enneagram, where the big issue is fear. Phobic Sixes are usually cautious, compliant, and dependent, and they consciously or unconsciously seek the protection of an authority figure. Counterphobic Sixes hide their fear behind an aggressive and challenging facade and rebel against authority. Most Sixes are a combination of phobic and counterphobic.

Sixes at Their BEST Are	Sixes at Their WORST Are
loyal	anxious
alert	controlling
curious	unpredictable
caring	paranoid
compassionate	defensive
witty	rigid
practical	testy
responsible	suspicious
supportive	sarcastic
honest	hypervigilant
reliable	cruel

Personality Inventory

Check what applies to you.

☐ 1 I am a loyal friend and partner.

☐ 2 I usually don't trust anyone I haven't known for a long time.

☐ 3 I am alert by nature.

☐ 4 I feel especially close to my partner when we are standing together against a common enemy or working for a common cause.

☐ 5 I am proud of my intellect.

☐ 6 I usually become very indecisive when stressed. (This applies especially to the phobic style.)

☐ 7 People sometimes complain that I am too reactive, defensive, and controlling. (This applies especially to the counterphobic style.)

☐ 8 In a major crisis, I usually overcome my self-doubt and anxiety.

☐ 9 I mistrust people who try to flatter me.

☐ 10 There's almost nothing I like less than pretension.

☐ 11 I am usually responsible, hardworking, conscientious, and precise.

☐ 12 I frequently examine or test the loyalty of my friends or partner.

☐ 13 People say I take things too seriously.

☐ 14 At my worst in an intimate relationship, I am either insecure and anxious (when phobic) or testy and confrontational (when counterphobic).

☐ 15 I either think things through very carefully before I take action or I boldly charge in.

☐ 16 I prefer what is proven and predictable over what is new and unknown.

☐ 17 I either look to others to give me direction or I completely ignore advice and do whatever I want.

☐ 18 I often obsess about the worst possible outcome.

☐ 19 When threatened, I either become anxious and seek protection or confront the danger head-on.

☐ 20 I can be cynical and sarcastic.

Which Subtype Applies to You?

You May Relate to One, Two, or All Three Subtypes

Within each type there are three subtypes, representing the three aspects of instinctual life: personal well-being (*self-preservation*), one-to-one relationships (*relational*), and community (*social*). These subtypes or instincts are largely expressed in unconscious ways as we go about life. For most of us, the importance of one or more subtype is exaggerated, though, and interferes with our growth.

Sixes cope with, and divert attention from, their fear and anxiety in the following ways, depending on their subtype. As they develop, they will move beyond these limitations and gain trust in themselves and the world.

Self-Preservation Sixes: "Ingratiating"

*If you're going to tell people
the truth, make them laugh,
or they'll kill you.*

　　—Billy Wilder

Those in the self-preservation subtype are sometimes referred to as warm Sixes because of their friendliness.

- I am responsible, loyal, and witty. I try to make sure that people like me because then I feel protected.

- I love opportunities to prove that I stand by my friends. The bonus is they'll stand by me when I need it.

- I evaluate carefully how authority figures perceive me so I can stay in, or get back in, their good graces.

- I can't help trying to be cordial, even when I'm angry with someone.

- I have many worries and doubts and look to others for assurance and protection.

- I analyze every ramification of every action I'm about to take in order not to make mistakes or to jeopardize my safety.

- I need to have a safe house and to feel protected from the outer world.

Relational Sixes: "Strength and Beauty"

- I am very energetic and competitive. I work hard to achieve my goals.

- I try to make myself strong (physically or intellectually) and attractive (sexually or aesthetically).

- I need to be sure either that people know me and care about me and will come to my aid, or that I am capable of defending myself.

Arnold: When people offend me, threaten me, or make me jealous, I may retaliate with sarcastic or caustic remarks hoping they will back off. I keep my body strong in case I need to defend myself.

Gerard: I try to impress people with my knowledge and logic. I test, provoke, and prove I'm tough when necessary. Sometimes I intimidate or fly into a rage. There are plenty of people who want to get the best of me, but they can't as long as I have my brain, my ability to persevere, and my passionate style.

Marilyn: When I feel insecure, victimized, or defenseless, I act seductive or helpless. I can be tough and intimidating, but I prefer to use my beauty to protect me.

Sonya: I own an art gallery. It's a position that gives me clout and makes me feel secure and strong. This fits me well since I am sensitive aesthetically. People admire me for my taste and success—at least I hope they do. I'm good at taking care of myself and my business, but I'm always afraid underneath.

Relational Sixes, especially males, are usually counterphobic and resemble Eights in many ways.

Social Sixes: "Duty"

Woe to him inside a non-conformist clique that doesn't conform to non-conformity.

—Eric Hoffer

- I'm in constant dialogue with a committee I carry around in my head. It's based on voices of authority from my family, school, and church. When I'm making a decision, I will refer to this committee to verify that I'm doing the right thing.

- I am loyal to those within my family or group and skeptical of outsiders.

- I either try to be conscientious and follow the rules or test and break them, preferably with the support of coconspirators.

- When those in charge tell me what to do, I either feel relieved that the responsibility for the decision has been taken off my shoulders, or I become annoyed.

- It is not safe to depend on any one individual. I'd rather put my trust and support in a group or a cause.

- I am anxious about promotions. I want to succeed, but I worry about having serious responsibilities. I am also reluctant to take on a highly visible role where I might be ridiculed or criticized, as I do to my superiors.

- I have idealized a leader or a boss and later felt disillusioned.

- I can work untiringly for a cause I believe in.

Wings

Wings are the types on each side of your number. Sixes with a strong Five wing tend to be serious and studious, while Sixes with a strong Seven wing tend to be outgoing and active.

Sixes with a strong Five wing tend to be intellectually oriented, original, idiosyncratic, quiet, reclusive, negative, contentious, and arrogant. Sixes with a strong Seven wing tend to be sociable, ingratiating, playful, materialistic, manic, overreactive, and irritable.

Occasionally people present the persona of one of their wings—rather than their actual type—to the outside world.

Arrows

Your personality is also influenced by the two types that are connected to yours by lines, the *arrows* of Three and Nine.

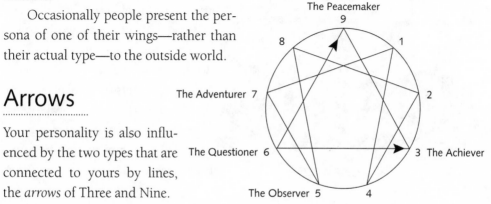

How Wings and Arrows Influence Your Behavior in Relationships

We have a natural connection to our wings and arrows. They often come into play without our knowing it: in a positive way when we're feeling tranquil and integrated, and in a negative way during times of stress. When we want to change something about ourselves, we can try consciously to incorporate their favorable and avoid their negative traits. You may want to read the chapters on Fives, Sevens, Threes, and Nines to learn more about your wings and arrows.

Sixes are surrounded by the other head-center types, Five and Seven, and are sometimes accused by their partner as being too "mental."

If you want to develop your introversion, you may do well to emulate your perceptive, soft-spoken Five wing. Be aware of the influence this wing can exert on you to be secretive, cynical, or suspicious, however.

If you want to develop your extroversion, call on your Seven wing to bring out your ability to be lively and spontaneous. You may wish to turn this wing off if you start to become too frenzied or impulsive.

If you are overly anxious or controlling, you can emulate your Nine arrow to acquire a calmer attitude. It can help you to trust and accept instead of suspecting other people's motives. Be careful not to become apathetic or habit-bound or to numb out with work, drugs, food, or alcohol.

Following your Three arrow, you can become secure, optimistic, and active, work and play hard, and make decisions more easily. Be aware of trying to impress people, however. Unless your partner is extremely busy or antisocial, he or she will prefer that you don't become a workaholic.

Healthy Sixes are responsible, witty, and compassionate. As friends and partners they are also warm, supportive, and loyal. When they develop trust, they are able to let go of anxiety and free up a lot of energy.

Characteristics of Sixes as Seen in Famous People

Speculations by the Authors

Anxious (phobic): Diane Keaton, Teri Garr, George on *Seinfeld*, Miles on *Murphy Brown*

I'm not afraid to die.
I just don't want to be there
when it happens.
    —Woody Allen

Daring (counterphobic): Evel Knieval, Napoleon, G. Gordon Liddy

Cerebral: Sigmund Freud, Charles Darwin, Krishnamurti

Dedicated to a cause: Attorney General Janet Reno, Oliver North, Robert Kennedy

Pessimistic: raconteur Oscar Levant

Pessimist—one who,
when he has the choice of
two evils, chooses both.
    —Oscar Wilde

Confrontational: Spike Lee, Malcolm X, Dabney Coleman

Looking for clues: Lieutenant Columbo, Marcia Clark

Paranoid: Senator Joseph McCarthy, President Richard M. Nixon, J. Edgar Hoover

Loyal: Michael in *The Godfather*

Warm and friendly: Ellen Degeneres, Duke Ellington, Jack Lemmon, Loretta Lynn

Sharp-witted: Mort Sahl, George Carlin, Jay Leno, Sid Caesar, Gene Wilder, Don Rickles, David Letterman, Charles Grodin

Devil's advocates: Phil Donahue, Andy Rooney

Masculine or feminine ideals: Mel Gibson, Robert Redford, Julia Roberts, Marilyn Monroe

Famous Pairs

Six and One: Mel Brooks and Anne Bancroft

Six and Two: Bob and Emily on *The Bob Newhart Show*

Six and Three: Mary and Ted on *The Mary Tyler Moore Show*

Six and Four: Princess Diana and Prince Charles

Six and Five: Woody Allen and Mia Farrow

Six and Six: Woody Allen and Diane Keaton in *Annie Hall*

Six and Seven: Meg Ryan and Dennis Quaid

Six and Eight: Billy Crystal and Jack Palance in *City Slickers*

Six and Nine: Warren Beatty and Annette Bening

Questioners in Relationships

*A pessimist is one who feels bad
when he feels good for fear he'll feel
worse when he feels better.*

—Anonymous

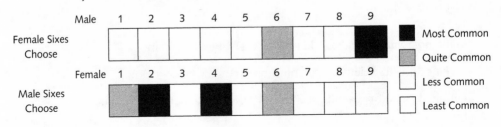

What Sixes Say About Ones (Perfectionists)

I like Ones because they

- are loyal and make me feel secure

- help me to prioritize and make decisions

- back me up when I get into a conflict with someone

- are hardworking and capable

- are highly principled

I have trouble with Ones because they

- have rigid expectations of how everyone and everything should be
- seethe instead of telling me what is bothering them, which makes my paranoid imagination go wild
- exacerbate my worrying by fretting so much
- scrutinize everything I do
- blame me for the problems we have

What Sixes Say About Twos (Helpers)

I like Twos because they

- envelop me in their warmth and give me a safe feeling
- joke around and help me to lighten up
- value my protectiveness
- try to help and do things right
- help me appreciate myself
- make everyone feel comfortable

I have trouble with Twos because they

- hate it when I confront them about my suspicions
- act friendly to people they dislike, so I worry they might be insincere with me
- activate my paranoia when they seem close one minute and distant the next
- don't always think things through carefully

What Sixes Say About Threes (Achievers)

I like Threes because they

- are hardworking, competent, and practical
- go straight for their goals and encourage me to go for mine

- look out for themselves

- see the future as bright

- encourage me to try new activities

I have trouble with Threes because they

- take my fears, worries, and doubts too lightly

- don't have enough time for our relationship, since they're so busy working and trying to succeed

- are not always honest; they sometimes put on acts in order to impress people

- keep busy to avoid their anxieties and have no patience for mine

What Sixes Say about Fours (Romantics)

I like Fours because they

- are usually bright, perceptive, and creative

- have high ideals and worthy principles

- are funny, ironic, clever, and imaginative

- like to deflate authority and pomposity, as I do

- have great emotional depth and stimulate my feelings

I have trouble with Fours because they

- isolate themselves from me and give me mixed messages; they can be loving one minute and rejecting the next

- become depressed or wounded easily, even over trifles

- try to make me feel guilty for hurting their feelings

- can be contrary, attacking, blaming, and obstinate

What Sixes Say About Fives (Observers)

I like Fives because they

- are objective and help me put my problems in perspective

- understand my fears and share in my intellectual interests; our wing relationship and being in the same head center give us a lot in common

- can be soft, tender, and nonjudgmental

- are loyal to their commitments

- remain calm and collected when I am in crisis

I have trouble with Fives because they

- don't always like to talk problems through with me

- feel burdened by my needs and distance themselves from me

- become sulky

- are so quiet I don't know what they're thinking; naturally I imagine the worst

- often seem indifferent or remote

What Sixes Say About Sixes

When everyone is out to get you,
paranoia is only good thinking.

　　—Johnny Fever, *WKRP in Cincinnati*

I like Sixes because we

- can have stimulating discussions together

- understand each other's fears and anxieties

- are willing to take unpopular stands

- use humor to get us through difficulties

- are clearly committed to our relationship and mutual security

- are forthright, aboveboard, and *loyal*

I have trouble with Sixes because we

- reinforce each other's negative and suspicious nature

- both turn everything into a catastrophe

- doubt almost everything

- are both unpredictable yet crave predictability

- both have trouble making up our minds

What Sixes Say About Sevens (Adventurers)

I like Sevens because they

- balance my doubting mind by expecting the best from the future

- entertain me and help me lighten up

- introduce me to fascinating new ideas

- encourage me to try new things and move out of my fears

- are idealistic

I have trouble with Sevens because they

- don't want to hear about my fears or other "negative" issues

- make me anxious and jealous when they go places without me

- are too busy and self-absorbed to have time for our relationship

- make me feel even more like a worrier, given their optimism

I'm a kind of paranoid in reverse. I suspect people of plotting to make me happy.
      —J. D. Salinger

What Sixes Say About Eights (Asserters)

I like Eights because they

- don't worry about what others think of them

- shoot down others' pretensions

- act in my behalf and protect me

- tell me exactly where they stand so I don't have to guess and worry

- are confident—they make bold decisions and take charge

I have trouble with Eights because they

- regard tender feelings as weakness

- are as strong-willed as I am, so we lock horns hopelessly in arguments

- have no tolerance for my fretting or indecisiveness

- try to boss me around

What Sixes Say About Nines (Peacemakers)

I like Nines because they

- listen to me when I unload my fears

- help me feel secure by accepting me for who I am

- encourage me to see things from a broad perspective

- are even-tempered and comfortable
to be with; it's easier for me to
access my Nine arrow and relax
when I'm with a healthy Nine
friend or lover

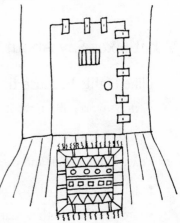

I have trouble with Nines because they

- become obstinate or passive-aggressive
when angry instead of being direct

- criticize me for taking too many precautions

- tune me out at times and leave me feeling insecure and alone

- are not always active enough; I like to keep moving

- do not take the initiative, so I don't know what they really want

Things Sixes Would Never Dream of Doing . . .

☞ remaining totally optimistic and calm when their partner is three hours late from an afternoon of skydiving

☞ relaxing all weekend long, secure in the knowledge that they will do just fine when their new job begins on Monday

☞ enduring a two-week guided tour with twelve chattering, flattering, giggling busybodies

☞ being certain that they are the perfect teacher for the Power of Positive Thinking class

☞ forgetting the head of the company's name when introducing him or her at the stockholders' meeting and laughing it off

☞ going directly to their boss with a major grievance and not first soliciting support from co-workers

☞ sitting in the first row of the balcony at the theater and not wondering if the railing is strong enough to lean on

How to Get Along with Sixes

I just want you to love me, primal doubts and all.

—Max Schumacher in *Network*

- Appreciate their loyalty, intellect, compassion, wit, and their ability to come through in emergencies or crisis situations.

- Encourage them to move on to more constructive thoughts and projects when they have a problem that can't be resolved.

- Reassure them of your commitment to the relationship.

- Be open and honest. They feel safer when all the cards are on the table.

- Make clear agreements with them that leave no room for doubt.

- Don't flatter them, act overly nice, or beat around the bush.

- When in conflict, let them know that you are looking for a way to resolve the matter constructively.

- If they go into a rage, back off and let their anger wind down; reacting angrily or fearfully only adds fuel to the fire.

- Encourage them to talk about their fears. Listen without trying to fix what's bothering them.

- But be honest and sensitive if their anxieties begin to drive you up the wall.

- Encourage them to get reality checks when hurt or offended by asking the offender what he or she really meant.

You can give Sixes extra support in these ways:

- Encourage them to get plenty of exercise to help prevent and relieve anxiety and stress.

- Encourage them to stop thinking and to take action when appropriate.

- Show them that some options require measured risk.

- Help them focus on the best things that could happen rather than on the worst.

- Urge them to learn to trust their own decisions and to trust what each moment brings.

Jim and Joan are going with the current.

THE

ADVENTURER

When choosing between two evils,
I always like to take the one I've never tried before.
—Mae West

Sevens are motivated by the need to be happy, to contribute to the world, and to avoid pain and suffering.

Fives, Sixes, and Sevens constitute the head center of the Enneagram and respond to fear in very different ways. Sevens deny or suppress anxiety by making lots of plans and by keeping busy.

Sevens at Their BEST Are	Sevens at Their WORST Are
enthusiastic	self-centered
energetic	impulsive
lively	rebellious
fun-loving	manic
spontaneous	restless
imaginative	opinionated
charming	defensive
curious	distracted
lighthearted	unreliable
generous	self-destructive

I feel tied down.

Fine, then leave! But I get the frequent-flyer coupons!

Personality Inventory

Check what applies to you.

☐ 1 I am optimistic, outgoing, and good at doing many things.

☐ 2 I look for new, intriguing experiences.

☐ 3 I like relationships that are exciting and intense yet steady and dependable.

☐ 4 I want to live the good life, which includes delicious food and plenty of fun and adventure.

☐ 5 I have difficulty with people when they are needy, dependent, and negative.

☐ 6 I usually recover quickly from losses.

☐ 7 I love getting attention and laughs for telling good stories and jokes.

☐ 8 I support people by getting them out of their bad moods and negativity.

☐ 9 I worry about having my freedom curtailed.

☐ 10 I don't like feeling obligated or beholden to anyone.

☐ 11 As a thinking type, I usually don't like to listen to people process feelings. As a feeling type, I can take an interest in this kind of thing unless the person keeps repeating the same misery and does nothing to change it.

☐ 12 I have a lot of friends and acquaintances.

☐ 13 I sometimes feel shy, vulnerable, and fragile inside, but others think I am always confident.

☐ 14 Most people find me friendly, attractive, and charming.

☐ 15 Sometimes I am self-indulgent and engage in excesses.

☐ 16 I can be defensive and argumentative.

☐ 17 I make more plans than I actually carry out.

☐ 18 I usually find ways to evade confrontations in daily life.

☐ 19 I like to say the unexpected.

☐ 20 If I want to end a relationship, I am likely either to confront directly or to get the person to leave me by irritating him or her.

Which Subtype Applies to You?

You May Relate to One, Two, or All Three Subtypes

Within each type there are three subtypes, representing the three aspects of instinctual life: personal well-being (*self-preservation*), one-to-one relationships (*relational*), and community (*social*). These subtypes or instincts are largely expressed in unconscious ways as we go about life. For most of us, the importance of one or more subtypes is exaggerated, though, and this interferes with our growth.

Sevens deny their fear of pain and suffering. They do so in the following ways, according to their subtype. As they develop, they move beyond these limitations and become more grounded and realistic.

Self-Preservation Sevens: "Family and Like-Minded Friends"

Self-preservation Sevens tend to be more family oriented than the other subtypes.

- I like having a home base where we share values and interests and provide a network of support for each other.

- I often take the role of keeping people entertained and happy.

- Planning for and reminiscing about an adventure is usually at least as thrilling as the adventure itself.

- I prefer my friends to be positive, as I am.

- I like to be spontaneous, but I also plan ahead to make sure I will see my friends and not miss out on anything.

- When I take risks, they are usually measured rather than reckless.

- I spend a lot of time in and around my house.

Relational Sevens: "Excitement"

The devil's name is dullness.

　—Robert E. Lee

- I like challenge and action.

- Sometimes I push things to the edge or step on people's toes.

- I prefer whatever is unusual, intense, complex, or aesthetically pleasing.

- Sometimes I am seductive without meaning to be and get more entangled than I had intended.

- I pursue fascinating people and adventures.

- When a relationship loses its charge, I may romanticize the person to avoid boredom, or, if I feel trapped, I back away.

- I can become upset over the discrepancy between the ideal relationship and reality.

- It makes me unhappy if my partner doesn't fully experience excitement and adventure with me.

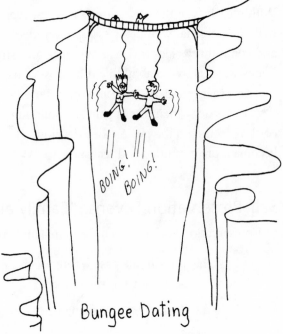

Bungee Dating

Social Sevens: "Impatient vs. Idealistic"

- I can see myself risking my life for a principle or cause I believe in.

- Sometimes I'm slow to act on my good intentions, especially when I would have to give up some freedom.

- I try to stifle my longings for adventure and put responsibilities to my family, career, or a cause first.

- I don't like the burden of feeling responsible for the people around me.

- I like companionship and brotherhood, but I can't stand it when anyone tries to control or coerce me.

- I can be impatient. I want to take action right now instead of wasting time bickering about procedures.

- Inequality among people upsets me. I wish there didn't have to be pecking orders.

- I have a large circle of friends.

- I like to keep up on what is new in the community

Wings

Wings are the types on each side of your number. Their Six wing influences Sevens to appear fidgety and lighthearted. When their Eight wing is dominant, Sevens have a more grounded feeling and are more in touch with anger.

Sevens with a strong Six wing tend to be sensitive, ingratiating, committed, dutiful, anxious, insecure, easily hurt, and hesitant.

Sevens with a strong Eight wing tend to be powerful, assertive, impatient, gregarious, hedonistic, boisterous, self-centered, and unfaithful.

Occasionally people present the persona of one of their wings—rather than their actual type—to the outside world.

Arrows

Your personality is also influenced by the two types that are connected to yours by lines, the *arrows* of One and Five.

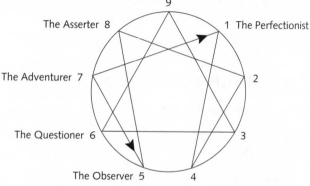

How Wings and Arrows Influence Your Behavior in Relationships

We have a natural connection to our wings and arrows, and they come into play without our knowing it: their positive aspects when we're feeling tranquil and integrated, and their unhealthy aspects during times of stress. When we want to change something about ourselves, we can try consciously to incorporate their favorable and avoid their negative traits. You may want to read the chapters on Sixes, Eights, Fives, and Ones and learn more about them.

The Seven and its wings are among the most energetic types on the Enneagram. Your Six wing can influence you to be loyal, responsible, and affectionate. Be aware of being overly dependent, as phobic Sixes can be, or overly controlling, as counterphobic Sixes can be. Keep in mind that Sixes are likely to swing back and forth from one characteristic to its opposite.

Your Eight wing can be a source of great exuberance and of discovering adventure in opposition. It can influence you to be more competitive, self-confident, and goal oriented. Be careful not to issue commands to your partner, though.

Your Five arrow can encourage you to accept the polarities of good and bad, happy and sad, and to become more moderate and self-disciplined. There may be a tendency, though, to withdraw into your mind, detach when in conflict, or push theories onto people.

You can learn to stay grounded and weigh your options wisely when you access your One arrow. But be careful not to lose your optimistic attitude, and avoid becoming overly self-critical, faultfinding, irritable, or blaming.

Healthy Sevens make adventure-sharing, productive partners. They model generosity, optimism, and cheerfulness, and they inspire those around them to feel good. In addition, developed Sevens are supportive and help loved ones fulfill their potential.

Characteristics of Sevens as Seen in Famous People and Roles

Speculations by the Authors

Lead me not into temptation.
I can find the way myself.

—Rita Mae Brown

Upbeat: Martin Short, Robin Williams, Chevy Chase, Goldie Hawn, Carol Burnett, Tim Allen, Dave Barry, Gene Kelly, Geena Davis, Leslie Nielsen, Eddie Murphy, Kevin Kline, Dizzy Gillespie

Idealistic: John F. Kennedy, Henry David Thoreau

Optimistic: Auntie Mame, Ruth Gordon as Maude in *Harold and Maude*

Free-spirited: Hawkeye on *M.A.S.H.,* Jack on *Three's Company*

Pleasure-seeking or self-obsessed: Zsa Zsa Gabor, Luciano Pavarotti, Liberace, Leonard Bernstein, Blanche on *The Golden Girls,* Alexis on *Dynasty*

A lot of people may not know this,
but I'm quite famous.
   —Sam Malone, *Cheers*

Eternally young: Tom Smothers, W. A. Mozart, Peter Pan, Saint-Exupéry's Little Prince

Spiritual seekers: Ram Dass, Joseph Campbell

Multi-talented: Peter Ustinov, Shirley MacLaine, Steve Martin, Lily Tomlin, Leonardo da Vinci, Dudley Moore, Steve Allen, Sam Francis

I've had a wonderful life.
I took a crack at everything.
   —Vincent Price

Innovative: Gene Roddenberry (originator of *Star Trek*), Robert Altman, Federico Fellini, Steven Spielberg, Kurt Vonnegut

Money doesn't matter to me,
curiosity does.
   —Barry Diller

Adventurous: George Plimpton, Indiana Jones, James Bond

Probing: Jim Lehrer, Charlie Rose

Debonair: David Niven, Michael Caine, Errol Flynn

Bouncy: basketball great Michael Jordan

Famous Pairs

Seven and One: Sam Malone and Diane Chambers on *Cheers*

Seven and Two: Mork and Mindy

Seven and Three: Goldie Hawn and Kurt Russell

Seven and Four: Rhett Butler and Scarlett O'Hara in *Gone with the Wind*

Seven and Five: *Melvin and Howard* (Melvin Dummar and Howard Hughes)

Seven and Six: Louis Malle and Candice Bergen

Seven and Seven: Lucille Ball and Desi Arnaz on *I Love Lucy*

Seven and Eight: Rita Mae Brown and Martina Navratilova

Seven and Nine: Peg and Al Bundy on *Married . . . with Children*

Adventurers in Relationships

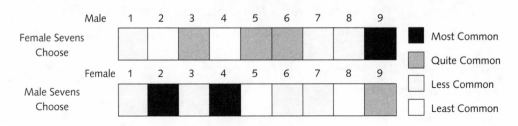

What Sevens Say About Ones (Perfectionists)

I like Ones because they

- provide me with a safe and stable refuge from my hectic lifestyle

- have energy and determination and set a good example for me of persevering and completing what they start

- enjoy the kind of disciplined work that I don't have patience for: paying bills, going over the checking account, and the like

- are principled and support worthwhile causes
- appreciate the *balance* my optimistic and carefree personality brings to our relationship

I have trouble with Ones because they

- are righteous, give me critical and judgmental frowns, and try to make me feel guilty
- believe the world is flawed and needs to be fixed—*their* way
- worry and get depressed instead of enjoying life; they become fixated on their inner pain when they move toward their Four arrow
- tell me what I should do and how I should live

What Sevens Say About Twos (Helpers)

I like Twos because they

- share enthusiastically in my adventures and in my joy of life
- are comfortable expressing emotions and help me to express mine
- give me plenty of attention
- understand my need for freedom (up to a point)
- see my potential and help me fulfill my dreams
- can become interested in many things

I have trouble with Twos because they

- sulk or get angry when I am unable to listen to them

- obsess about our relationship instead of just going about their life

- try to butter me up, change me, and pin me down on things

- need to be more direct about expressing what they want

- compete with me for attention

What Sevens Say About Threes (Achievers)

I like Threes because they

- are dynamic and have enough energy to keep up with me

- are gregarious, upbeat, and adventurous

- are industrious, self-reliant, and committed to their goals

- give me the freedom to do my own thing

- like themselves

I have trouble with Threes because they

- are too involved in projects and unavailable for our relationship

- are attached to staying optimistic, as I am, so important issues between us get swept under the rug

- can't be counted on to show up for the special plans I make
- base their behavior on the effect it will have on others

What Sevens Say About Fours (Romantics)

I like Fours because they

- like to be in the midst of passion, intensity, and excitement
- have fascinating inner worlds and teach me how to explore mine
- appreciate the special things life has to offer
- don't like to conform any more than I do
- appreciate me for introducing them to unusual activities

I have trouble with Fours because they

- get emotional and blow things out of proportion
- are often too down to have fun with me
- can become an emotional drag
- have a slower pace than I do, especially those with a Five wing
- try to control me

What Sevens Say About Fives (Observers)

I like Fives because they

- are unconventional, interesting, and knowledgeable in many areas
- have an inner strength that I admire
- have consuming interests and understand my need to pursue mine

- are good models of how to concentrate on one thing at a time
- don't tug at me

I have trouble with Fives because they

- are less interested in new adventures than I am; they can be happy doing the same thing over and over
- criticize me for being too exuberant and frantic
- want to be alone when I want to have our friends over
- put up a wall, pout, and won't talk when they're offended
- can be too picky

What Sevens Say About Sixes (Questioners)

I like Sixes because they

- like to laugh with me
- are curious, alert, and challenge me mentally
- are warm and understanding, especially the feeling types
- are active and playful, especially those with strong Seven wings
- are loyal

I have trouble with Sixes because they

- drive me crazy trying to think of every single possibility before they make a decision
- make me want to run out of the room when they become fearful, argumentative, or controlling
- criticize me for being self-indulgent
- see negativity everywhere they look and fly off the handle over nothing
- are too rigid and duty-bound

What Sevens Say About Sevens

I like Sevens because we

- match each other's energy (most people can't keep up with us)
- like frequent, brief contacts

- share interests and a vision for a better world
- are both independent
- have fun together making and carrying out plans for adventures

I have trouble with Sevens because we

- don't always listen to each other

Enough about me, let's talk about you.
What do you think about me?

  —Anonymous

- can both be overly critical and overly sensitive
- look the other way when problems come up
- each like to flirt and get all the attention
- both are intent on maintaining our freedom

It might be a shaky marriage—
they're BOTH missing the
commitment chromosome!

What Sevens Say About Eights (Asserters)

I like Eights because they

- like to take the devil's advocate position and have intense discussions with me
- protect the underdog
- stick to their guns in defending their ideals
- know how to let loose and kick up their heels

- are independent, self-reliant, and give me room to do my own thing
- call a spade a spade

I have trouble with Eights because they

- give me orders and insist that I see things their way
- cut people out of their life permanently and leave me to wonder if I might be next
- have angry outbursts
- fill up the whole room with their personality, and no one else gets heard
- dismiss what I have to say or don't listen in the first place

What Sevens Say About Nines (Peacemakers)

I like Nines because they

- are easygoing and fun to hang out with
- don't like confrontation any more than I do
- are accepting and nonjudgmental; they don't get upset when I'm a little late, for instance
- appreciate my idealism

- like to listen to my stories and enjoy the good things in life with me
- give me plenty of attention

I have trouble with Nines because they

- tend to see the many options available, as I do, so we have trouble settling on what we're going to do
- can be too stubborn
- resist doing new things that would interrupt their routines
- often don't follow through and don't do what they say they will do
- seem to be in slow motion most of the time

Things Sevens Would Never Dream of Doing . . .

☞ passing up an invitation to go on a trek in the Himalayas because they'd promised themselves they'd organize the garage

☞ going to a familiar restaurant when there was a new, exotic one next door

☞ choosing the dullest person at the seminar to take breaks with

☞ doing any one thing over and over

☞ deciding on an exact itinerary for their entire vacation
and following it steadfastly

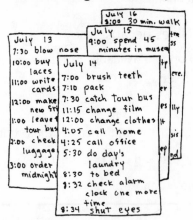

☞ taking the job of inspecting government forms to see if
there are any misprints

How to Get Along with Sevens

- Appreciate their optimism, spontaneity, and enthusiasm for new experiences.

- Listen to their stories, engage with them in stimulating conversation, and join
them in fun and adventures.

- Don't try to box them into schedules and routines.

Ann likes to keep her plans flexible
and open to last-minute changes.

- Be gentle with criticism. Make it brief and put it in a way that doesn't make them feel defensive.

- Develop plenty of interests of your own rather than depending on them for all your companionship and entertainment.

- If they talk too much for you and you begin to feel like their audience, try to make the discussion a two-way exchange. If this doesn't work, excuse yourself diplomatically and do something else.

- Hold back on analyzing and processing feelings with them, especially if you are a feeling type and they are a thinking type.

- Since Sevens tend to deny and gloss over difficulties, remind them that the same problems will keep recurring if not addressed.

- Step back and detach if they seem overly rude or brash and it isn't your style to confront; but don't let them off the hook altogether.

You can give Sevens extra support in these ways:

- Remind them to stay with their feelings and recognize their fear. Be with them in it.

- Encourage them to do regular physical exercise.

- Help them learn to hang in and express resentment.

- Encourage them to experience the full range of emotions: joy and pain, pleasure and sorrow.

Vladimir learned the value of patience, moderation, and building for the future.

And then he went skydiving.

THE

ASSERTER

Never settle with words what you can accomplish with a flame-thrower.
—Bruce Feirstein

Eights are motivated by the need to be self-reliant, strong, and to make an impact on the world.

Eights, Nines, and Ones constitute the gut center and have issues that revolve around self-forgetting and anger. Eights lose touch with themselves and follow the role of enforcer. Unlike Nines and Ones, they readily express anger.

Eights at Their BEST Are	Eights at Their WORST Are
confident	insensitive
energetic	domineering
truthful	self-centered
decisive	overly aggressive
direct	demanding
loyal	arrogant
protective	combative
generous	possessive
supportive	uncompromising
brave	faultfinding

Personality Inventory

Check what applies to you.

☐ 1 I like excitement and stimulation and am attracted to intense people.

☐ 2 I may have a hard outer shell, but when I feel trusting, I can be vulnerable and loving.

☐ 3 People see me as courageous.

☐ 4 I can be tough and hard-driving.

☐ 5 People who are not as strong as I am are sometimes put off by my assertive and confrontational style.

☐ 6 In a committed relationship I am willing to go to any length to get to the bottom of conflicts.

☐ 7 Whether in an intimate relationship or not, I need some time alone.

☐ 8 My friends complain that I sometimes dismiss their point of view.

☐ 9 Independence and self-reliance are of utmost importance to me.

☐ 10 I demand fairness and equality.

☐ 11 I am extremely protective of my loved ones.

☐ 12 I usually have no problem saying what is on my mind.

☐ 13 I like to empower and motivate people.

☐ 14 I support the disadvantaged.

☐ 15 Sometimes I don't allow others to get close to me, because I don't want to be let down later.

☐ 16 I would rather be respected than liked.

☐ 17 I want things to be orderly and in their place, especially *my* things.

☐ 18 I have a tendency to indulge in excesses (food, drugs, etc.).

☐ 19 My first reaction is often to blame someone.

☐ 20 I like to shoot down pretension in people.

Which Subtype Applies to You?

You May Relate to One, Two, or All Three Subtypes

Within each type there are three subtypes, representing the three aspects of instinctual life: personal well-being (*self-preservation*), one-to-one relationships (*relational*), and community (*social*). These subtypes or instincts are usually expressed in unconscious ways as we go about life. For most of us, the importance of one or more subtypes is exaggerated, though, and this interferes with our growth.

Eights take charge and try to be powerful in the following ways, depending on their subtype. As they develop, they move beyond these limitations and have less need to prevail over others.

Self-Preservation Eights: "Satisfactory Survival"

The art of living is more like wrestling than dancing.
Stand firm and be ready for an unforeseen attack.

—Marcus Aurelius

- I keep myself supplied with plenty of food, comforts, and emergency supplies.

- Independence and security are very important to me; I don't want to rely on others for money or anything else.

- I get out of sorts when the details of my life are not in order and when access to what I am used to or want is cut off.

- A main theme in my life is protection—of myself, of my belongings, and of others.

- I feel safer when I sit where I can observe everything going on in the room.

- I try to make certain that no one will sneak up or intrude upon me.

Relational Eights: "Possession and Surrender"

Relational Eights, especially males, are the most excessive of all the subtypes.

- I am too assertive for some. I prefer high energy and intensity to the deadness of the comfort zone.

- My needs to possess and surrender are interwoven. I can be soft and vulnerable if I trust the person I am with, yet I never completely lose the impulse to command.

- I'm often in conflict about wanting a partner who needs to be taken care of versus wanting one I respect who will stand his or her ground against me.

- One way to get on my bad side is to neglect to consult me or ask my opinion about a matter that directly or indirectly involves me.

- It irritates me when people withhold their emotions or thoughts from me, especially when we are trying to work through a problem.

- I am attracted to people who are direct and who are not allergic to confrontation.

- I feel closer to my partner when we fight, because fighting brings out the truth, but constant arguing can burn me out of a relationship.

- I take precautions to make sure that no one tries to pull a power play on me or threaten my relationship.

Social Eights: "Friend or Foe?"

A true friend is one who sticks by you even when he gets to know you real well.

- I can't let my guard down until I know where I stand and that I'm respected.

- I test my friends for their loyalty. Once trust is firmly established, I usually stay in friendships for life.

- When in a group, I focus on who else has power in order to maintain my authority.

- I will go to bat for my friends and the weaker members of the community, but I want them to try to develop self-reliance and get back on their feet again.

- I try to be loyal and work problems out, but if someone walks over the line and betrays my trust, I may cut him or her out of my life forever.

- I love the excitement of a righteous struggle for truth or fairness.

- I usually take the role of protector in a group and make sure that justice is upheld.

Wings

Wings are the types on each side of your number. Eights with a strong Seven wing are among the most assertive of Enneagram types. Eights who lean toward type Nine tend to be quietly strong.

Eights with a strong Seven wing tend to be sociable, ambitious, impulsive, risk taking, aggressive, overreactive, materialistic, and prone to addiction.

Eights with a strong Nine wing tend to be steady, supportive, patient, modest, calmly dominating, slow to erupt with anger, cold, and indifferent.

This type often oscillates between being confrontational and conciliatory.

Occasionally people present the persona of one of their wings—rather than their actual type—to the outside world.

Arrows

Your personality is also influenced by the two types that are connected to yours by lines, the *arrows* of Two and Five.

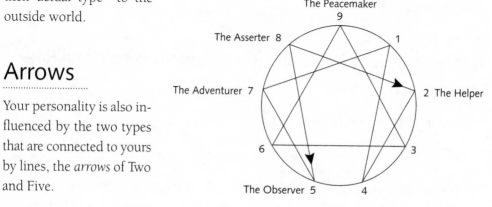

How Wings and Arrows Influence Your Behavior in Relationships

We have a natural connection to our wings and arrows, and they come into play without our knowing it: their positive aspects when we're feeling tranquil and integrated, and their unhealthy aspects during times of stress. When we want to change something about ourselves, we can try consciously to incorporate their favorable and to avoid their negative traits. You may want to read the chapters on Sevens, Nines, Twos, and Fives to learn more about them.

The Eight's wings, Seven and Nine, affect this type in very different ways. When your Seven wing is stronger, you are probably extroverted, energetic, and quick. On the negative side, this wing can influence you to be egocentric or hyperactive. The peaceful Nine and the aggressive Eight are probably the most contrasting of all the wing relationships. You can emulate your Nine wing in order to be more mild-mannered and receptive, but be aware of the influence it can have on you to take up other people's agendas and causes or to be stubborn and resistant.

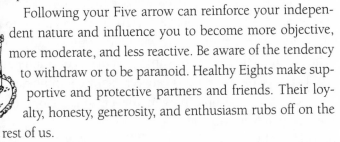

Your Two arrow specializes in relating successfully to people with warmth, tenderness, and compassion. Be aware of overdependence, possessiveness, and making unrealistic demands on people.

Following your Five arrow can reinforce your independent nature and influence you to become more objective, more moderate, and less reactive. Be aware of the tendency to withdraw or to be paranoid. Healthy Eights make supportive and protective partners and friends. Their loyalty, honesty, generosity, and enthusiasm rubs off on the rest of us.

Characteristics of Eights as Seen in Famous People and Roles

Speculations by the Authors

What I wanted to be when I grew up was—in charge.

　　—Brigadier General Wilma Vaught

Powerful and strong: Fidel Castro, Lyndon Johnson, Ann Richards, Indira Gandhi, Joseph Stalin, Golda Meir, Charles de Gaulle, George "Old Blood and Guts" Patton, Norman Schwarzkopf, Saddam Hussein, Martin Luther King, Jr.

As long as you're going to think anyway, think big.

  —Donald Trump

Outspoken: Germaine Greer, Bella Abzug, Ed Asner, Murphy Brown

Aggressive, pushy, or bullying: Rush Limbaugh, Marge Schott (president and CEO of the Cincinnati Reds), Frank Sinatra ("Chairman of the Board"), Jimmy Hoffa, Carla on *Cheers,* F. Lee Bailey, Marlon Brando in *The Godfather*

Larger than life: Davy Crockett, Kazantzakis's Zorba, Perry Mason

Protective: Curtis Sliwa (head of the Guardian Angels), Arnold Schwarzenegger in the *Terminator* films

Outrageous: John Belushi, Roseanne, Milton Berle

Gutsy: Mike Wallace, Pat Buchanan, Barbara Walters, Bea Arthur

Formidable: Pete Rose ("I never did anything halfway"), Charles Barkley, Billie Jean King, Mike Tyson, John McEnroe, George Foreman, Jim Brown, Mike Ditka

I hit big or miss big.
I live as big as I can.

  — Babe Ruth

Artistically forceful: Ernest Hemingway, Norman Mailer, Leo Tolstoy, John Ford

Famous Pairs

Eight and One: Humphrey Bogart and Lauren Bacall

Eight and Two: J. R. Ewing and Sue Ellen in *Dallas*

Eight and Three: W. C. Fields and Mae West in *My Little Chickadee*

Eight and Four: Aristotle Onassis and Maria Callas

Eight and Five: Michelle Pfeiffer and Jeff Bridges in *The Fabulous Baker Boys*

Eight and Six: Mao Zedong and Jiang Qing

Eight and Seven: Roseanne and Tom Arnold

Eight and Eight: Danny De Vito and Rhea Perlman

Eight and Nine: Lyndon and Lady Bird Johnson

Asserters in Relationships

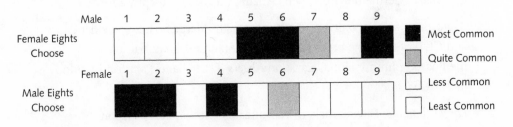

Male   1   2   3   4   5   6   7   8   9

Female Eights Choose

Female   1   2   3   4   5   6   7   8   9

Male Eights Choose

■ Most Common
▨ Quite Common
□ Less Common
□ Least Common

What Eights Say About Ones (Perfectionists)

I like Ones because they

- are intense; I feel charged around them

- stand up for themselves

- admire my courage and determination

- are practical, responsible, and don't let people down

- speak clearly, truthfully, and to the point

I have trouble with Ones because they

- are self-righteous and live by an inflexible set of rules

- can be pigheaded and try to control me

- are overzealous

- worry about what people think of them

- take offense at my bold language and behavior

- are sometimes unrealistic in their perceptions of themselves and others

What Eights Say About Twos (Helpers)

I like Twos because they

- relate to me openly and help me get in touch with the soft feelings I associate with my Two arrow

- are usually vivacious and enthusiastic

- have big hearts and make sacrifices for their family and friends

- give me generous attention

- appreciate my protection

I have trouble with Twos because they

- get cold and distant instead of standing up to me

- act phony and avoid controversy in order to get people to like and accept them

- try to get revenge when they don't get enough attention

- induce my guilt by acting hurt and wounded when I'm just being myself

- are too attached to being nice and trying to help me out

What Eights Say About Threes (Achievers)

I like Threes because they

- take the initiative and get things done

- work and play with great energy

- are optimistic

- appreciate my generosity

- usually recover quickly from setbacks

I have trouble with Threes because they

- withdraw when they're angry instead of having it out with me

- try to please everyone and offend no one

- do things to impress people instead of being their own person

- are too tied up with working and networking

- can't let go emotionally

What Eights Say About Fours (Romantics)

I like Fours because they

- match my energy and keep the intensity level high

- have a rebellious streak, as I do

- stand up for their ideals courageously

- appreciate my groundedness

- have interesting minds and emotional depth

- engage with me in healthy competition

I have trouble with Fours because they

- won't confront the people they have problems with

- get stuck in victimization

- take what I say too personally

- criticize my behavior

- make life complicated by constantly delving into their feelings and the meaning of life

What Eights Say About Fives (Observers)

I like Fives because they

- think things through intelligently and methodically

- are self-reliant and understand my need to be independent

- are inventive and witty

- see me as a role model for assertiveness

- admire my ability to be direct and to go for what I want

- are discreet—they can be trusted to keep things private

I have trouble with Fives because they

- withdraw or pout when they think I'm being too coarse or intense

- become vague and theorize instead of taking action; they often wiggle away instead of standing firm to meet me

- judge me for being a know-it-all and don't recognize it in themselves

- don't seem to value engagement, intensity, and liveliness

- can be dry, boring, and standoffish

- are impossible to budge when they have their minds made up

What Eights Say About Sixes (Questioners)

I like Sixes because they

- admire my courage

- appreciate my support

- want to be trusted and understand my need to trust them

- keep me on my toes in discussions

- offer me well-thought-out opinions

- have a flair for humor and make me laugh

- are loyal and back me up in hard times

I have trouble with Sixes because they

- try my patience with their excessive analyzing, talking, and deliberating

- don't trust themselves and therefore need to depend on others (when phobic)

- stew about scenarios that are probably never going to happen

- are afraid to try new things

- pressure me for reassurance

- either hold back too much or push forward in an ungrounded way

What Eights Say About Sevens (Adventurers)

I like Sevens because they

- say what they think and don't take themselves too seriously

- let loose, enjoy themselves, and make me laugh

- balk at authority

- have unlimited stamina for adventure and good times

- come up with exciting things for us to do

I have trouble with Sevens because they

- have zero tolerance for my anger

- are hard to approach when there are problems or conflicts

- are inconsistent in giving attention and support

- try to charm me into doing their dirty work (confronting people on their behalf, for example)

- rationalize, are indirect, and can be devious; this really annoys me because I'm a stickler for the truth

What Eights Say About Eights

I like Eights because we

- value each other's commitment to truth and justice, family and friends
- both are energetic and get all we can out of life
- play hard together, verbally and physically
- give each other plenty of challenge and plenty of love
- like the intensity of heated discussions

I have trouble with Eights because we

- pick on each other and fight too much
- cut each other out when hurt and have trouble getting back together
- are both overly possessive
- have trouble sharing control

What Eights Say About Nines (Peacemakers)

I like Nines because they

- are generous
- are comfortable to be around and to hang out with
- give me plenty of affection and attention
- appreciate my dynamic personality
- help me get back into balance when my anger gets the best of me
- accept my exuberant behavior (up to a point)

I have trouble with Nines because they

- put a wedge between us by refusing to lock horns with me; I like a good argument now and then
- expect me to guess what they are thinking instead of telling me directly
- are often too passive and ambivalent and won't face the issues

- dampen my enthusiasm with their stubbornness

- sit on their energy and aliveness

Things Eights Would Never Dream of Doing . . .

☞ waiting patiently in line at the supermarket while the checker chats on and on with customers or files her fingernails

☞ remaining calm and collected when their power mower comes back from the neighbor's broken

☞ passing up seconds and thirds on their favorite dish

☞ not retaliating, or not wanting to retaliate, when someone embarrasses or makes fun of them

☞ jumping at the chance to get the boss coffee every morning and acting coy, batting their eyelashes, and giggling daintily

☞ asking colleagues to hold their hand when they feel insecure at the corporate meeting

How to Get Along with Eights

- Meet them with intensity. Eights like energetic physical and mental contact.

- Appreciate their strength, self-reliance, and sense of justice.

- Be honest and direct. Tell them what's on your mind, and don't try to prevent them from saying what they think.

- Let them know if they really wounded you. They are often unaware of their impact on others.

- Stand up for yourself. Don't allow them to push you around or invalidate your point of view.

- Work toward compromises that allow you both to keep your self-esteem.

- If they go into a rage, back off and let their anger wind down. Reacting angrily or fearfully will fan the fire.

- Honor their need to be alone.

- Accept their blustery style up to a point. Don't assume that everything is a personal attack.

You can give Eights extra support in these ways:

- Encourage them to relax and exercise regularly to prevent and deal with stress.

- Ask them to listen to other people's points of view.

- Remind them that most people like to avoid confrontation.

- Help them to feel comfortable talking about their problems and sharing their vulnerability with you.

THE

PEACEMAKER

We live very close together. So, our prime purpose in this life is to help others. And if you can't help them, at least don't hurt them.

—The Dalai Lama

Nines are motivated by the need to live in harmony, to merge with others, and to avoid conflict. Of all the Enneagram types, they are the most likely to identify with the other types.

Eights, Nines, and Ones constitute the gut center and have issues revolving around anger and self-forgetting. Nines blend in, accommodate others, and forget their own real needs. They often express their anger unconsciously.

Nines at Their BEST Are	Nines at Their WORST Are
accepting	passive-aggressive (show hostility indirectly)
patient	stubborn
wise	apathetic
empathic	unassertive
kind	defensive
gentle	spaced-out
supportive	forgetful
nonjudgmental	obsessive
receptive	overly accommodating

Personality Inventory

Check what applies to you.

- [ ] 1 My friends say they feel relaxed, comfortable, and peaceful around me.
- [ ] 2 Making decisions is often difficult, as I can see all sides of an issue.
- [ ] 3 I try not to place demands on others and I become stubborn when people place demands on me.
- [ ] 4 Sometimes I feel more ambitious for my partner than for myself.
- [ ] 5 I tend to procrastinate.
- [ ] 6 I am more likely to feel depressed and lethargic than angry.
- [ ] 7 People like me because I am accepting, nonjudgmental, and unpretentious.
- [ ] 8 I am very attached to my habits and routines.
- [ ] 9 I am easily distracted.
- [ ] 10 I like to have time in each day to relax and let my mind wander.
- [ ] 11 I'd often rather accommodate my partner than stand up for myself or confront him or her.
- [ ] 12 I don't usually want all the attention to be on me.
- [ ] 13 I often distract myself from my problems instead of fixing them.
- [ ] 14 I am thought of as a good listener, but I don't concentrate on what people say as much as they think I do.
- [ ] 15 I have trouble choosing one option and letting go of all the rest.
- [ ] 16 People say I'm too passive and indecisive.
- [ ] 17 I often feel anxious, but others are usually not aware of it.
- [ ] 18 I believe that everything will work out in the long run.
- [ ] 19 I am not as competitive or concerned with status and prestige as many people are.
- [ ] 20 Physical comfort is very important to me.

Which Subtype Applies to You?

You May Relate to One, Two, or All Three Subtypes

The subtypes within each type represent the three aspects of instinctual life: personal well-being (*self-preservation*), one-to-one relationships (*relational*), and community (*social*). These subtypes or instincts are largely expressed in unconscious ways as we go about life. For most of us, the importance of one or more subtypes is exaggerated, though, and interferes with our growth.

Nines divert attention from anger in the following ways, depending on their subtype. As they develop and discover their real desires and priorities, their need to merge with others and repress anger will become less dominant.

Self-Preservation Nines: "Appetite"

*The first thing I remembered liking
that liked me back was food.*

—Rhoda Morgenstern, *Rhoda*

- I am very attached to my rituals of watching TV, reading, working on my computer, sleeping extra long, going to movies, and so on, and I feel anxious when anything interferes with them.

- I tend to neglect important tasks and responsibilities and focus on my habits instead.

- Food is prime in my life. Sometimes I use it to numb out, distract myself, and cover up my feelings.

- I like to collect objects and information.

- Sometimes I have trouble throwing things away because I can't decide which really matter to me.

- I try to meet my own needs by keeping my home, car, office, or purse supplied with whatever I might want.

Relational Nines: "Union"

- I like the feeling of being in union with a lover, family member, friend, mentor, famous person, guru, pet, nature, or the divine.

- When not in a relationship, I usually feel melancholy and yearn to be.

- I try to make my partner happy, both to avoid conflict and because his or her happiness will rub off on me.

- I am usually so focused on my companion that I fail to notice what is going on with me.

- When my partner places demands on me, I either become stubborn, go away emotionally, or go along so as not to make waves.

- I often blame others for things that are not right with my life.

- Sometimes I long to be more independent and discover my own priorities, desires, and aliveness.

- I can stay with my own feelings best when I have an open expanse of time alone.

Social Nines: "Participation/Nonparticipation"

- In addition to wanting to further causes, I join groups in order to structure my time, to soak up energy and become enlivened, to see how I can best fit in, and to discover where to direct myself.

- Though I gravitate toward groups, I sometimes feel ambivalent about whether I really want to belong.

- If someone becomes bossy or unpleasant, I often can't find the words to speak out, and I become stubborn or withdrawn instead.

- I often stay on the fringe. This keeps me from having to commit myself fully and from having to participate in conflicts.

- I bring my mediating skills and my ability to build consensus to groups.

- I often take the role of caretaker due to my tendency to want to be all things to all people.

- Since I automatically become involved in whatever floats by, I pick up nuances from others; but I'm slow to pick up and express what I myself feel.

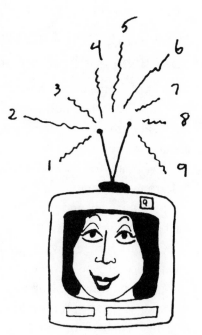

Wings

Wings are the types on each side of your number. Eight and One are in the same gut or anger center as the Nine. Eights lose touch with themselves and puff themselves up to feel powerful. Nines who have this wing developed can be effective leaders. With strong One wings, Nines are usually highly principled and hardworking.

Nines with a strong Eight wing tend to be willful, independent, lustful, steady, aggressive, competitive, and callous. This type often oscillates between being confrontational and conciliatory.

Nines with a strong One wing tend to be modest, composed, self-controlled, orderly, principled, obsessive-compulsive, and self-righteous.

Occasionally people present the persona of one of their wings—rather than their actual type—to the outside world.

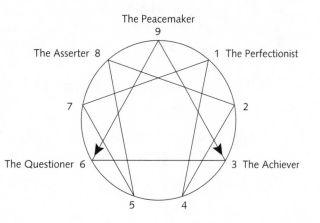

Arrows

Your personality is also influenced by the two types that are connected to yours by lines, the *arrows* of Three and Six.

How Wings and Arrows Influence Your Behavior in Relationships

We have a natural connection to our wings and arrows. They come into play without our knowing it: their positive aspects when we're feeling tranquil and integrated, and their unhealthy aspects during times of stress. When we want to change something about ourselves, we can try consciously to incorporate their favorable and avoid their negative traits. You may want to read the chapters on Eights, Ones, Threes, and Sixes to learn more about them.

Both the Eight and One wings can help the Nine to become more decisive and to establish strong boundaries.

Call on your Eight wing when you want to be more direct, outgoing, forceful, and independent. Using this wing to get your anger out in the open can be very healthful.

Your One wing can help you be more organized and get your chores done. When this wing is dominant, learn to express your feelings and desires, though, instead of holding them back, or your frustration may convert into indignation and resentment.

Your Three arrow can influence you to be practical, productive, focused, and confident; working with a purpose really feels great to a Nine. Be sure to follow your own meaningful goals, though, instead of becoming hyperactive or working to impress others.

Following the Six arrow, you can be more honest and outspoken. Your friends and partner will appreciate your loyalty. Your challenge at Six is to keep from being overwhelmed by anxiety and to avoid indecisiveness and blaming.

Healthy Nines are known for being laid back, even tempered, and nonjudgmental. They make people feel comfortable and are appreciated for their diplomacy, their wisdom, and their ability to form a solid union.

Characteristics of Nines as Seen in Famous People and Roles

Speculations by the Authors

Easygoing and likable: Jimmy Stewart, John Goodman on *Roseanne*

Gentle and kind: Audrey Hepburn

Fair and just: Abraham Lincoln

Accepting: Carl Rogers

Spiritual: Mahatma Gandhi, the Dalai Lama

Mellow: Bing Crosby, Perry Como, Mel Torme, Jerry Garcia, Johnny Mathis, Tony Bennett, Willie Nelson

Mellow-dious: Johannes Brahms

Easily distracted: Gracie Allen, Hugh Grant in *Four Weddings and a Funeral*, Rose on *The Golden Girls*

Political: Dwight D. Eisenhower, Gerald Ford

Accommodating: Judge Lance Ito

Wise and learned: Carl G. Jung

Comical: John Candy, Tim Conway, Garry Shandling, John Cleese

Articulate and friendly: Hugh Downs, Walter Cronkite, Garrison Keillor

Good mixer: Julia Child

Famous Pairs

Nine and One: Bill and Hillary Clinton

Nine and Two: Michael Douglas and Glenn Close in *Fatal Attraction*

Nine and Three: Loni Anderson and Burt Reynolds

Nine and Four: Edie Brickell and Paul Simon

Nine and Five: Henry and Margaret in *Howards End*

Nine and Six: Edith and Archie Bunker in *All in the Family*

Nine and Seven: Dan Rowen and Dick Martin

Nine and Eight: Gena Rowlands ("We actors can't stand to be just one person") and John Cassavetes

Nine and Nine: George Burns and Gracie Allen

Peacemakers in Relationships

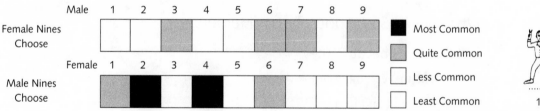

Male	1	2	3	4	5	6	7	8	9
Female Nines Choose			▨			▨	▨		▨

Female	1	2	3	4	5	6	7	8	9
Male Nines Choose	▨	■		■		▨			

■ Most Common
▨ Quite Common
☐ Less Common
☐ Least Common

147

What Nines Say About Ones (Perfectionists)

I like Ones because they

- model how to get clear about my purposes

- provide me with structure, activity, and definition

- form a connection with me that is stable and strong

- have a good sense of humor, especially healthy Ones

- are highly principled

- are loyal and do what they say they'll do

I have trouble with Ones because they

- have a hard time relaxing with me

- drive me nuts by criticizing, arguing, and stewing about things

- worry and obsess over details and unimportant matters

- admire my peacefulness yet try to speed me up

- become spiteful when I fall short of their expectations

- can be controlling, which forces me to be devious at times

What Nines Say About Twos (Helpers)

I like Twos because they

- make me feel important and loved

- are playful and lively

- make our home cozy and comfortable

- see the best in me and give me encouragement

- like physical attention

I have trouble with Twos because they

- complain or get angry when I don't do what they expect of me

- try to get me to do what they want by making me feel guilty

- get upset when they think I am not living up to my potential or taking enough initiative

- get angry, close down, or withhold their love if they feel ignored or offended

- attempt to wring my feelings out of me

What Nines Say About Threes (Achievers)

I like Threes because they

- show me a good example of setting goals and completing them

- initiate activities for us to do together

- are gregarious, optimistic, and self-assured

- have enough energy to carry out projects that I might just dream about

I have trouble with Threes because they

- rattle me by always being in a hurry
- don't give me enough contact; they can rarely relax and enjoy the moment with me
- criticize me for being too laid back and not working as hard as they do
- can be boastful and egotistical

What Nines Say About Fours (Romantics)

I like Fours because they

- listen to what I have to say
- make me feel important
- are compassionate and try to make the world a better place
- help me to get more in touch with my feelings
- appreciate the beauty of life
- let me in on their special world

I have trouble with Fours because they

- are too negative and self-absorbed; their melancholy and bitterness push me away
- focus on what is missing instead of on what is good in our lives
- accuse, blame, and try to change me
- upset me by overdramatizing things
- find me too mild and boring

What Nines Say About Fives (Observers)

I like Fives because they

- are soft-spoken and gentle
- listen to what I say, mull it over, then give me a well-thought-out response
- share their unusual perspective and vision with me

- do not make unnecessary demands or put pressure on me
- like to be together without having to talk all the time

I have trouble with Fives because they

- keep to themselves too much; I want a partner who likes to be with me

- make me feel unimportant when they withhold their feelings and thoughts from me

- hurt me by being too critical and abrupt

- don't initiate activities

- withdraw, detach, and disappear

What Nines Say About Sixes (Questioners)

I like Sixes because they

- appreciate my calmness

- are loyal; I feel sure they'll stay with me over the long haul

- can be very funny, playful, affectionate, and warm

- are competent or knowledgeable in many areas

- sympathize with me when I feel anxious or frantic

I have trouble with Sixes because they

- are often bothered by my quietness

- try to get a reaction out of me or control me

- look for hidden meanings behind what I say

- blame me for everything that goes wrong, can be unforgiving, and freak me out with their paranoia

- turn everything that happens into a big deal

One way to get high blood pressure is
to go mountain climbing over molehills.

　　　　—Earl Wilson

What Nines Say About Sevens (Adventurers)

I like Sevens because they

- have a positive outlook

- make activities lively and fun; I love getting swept up in their enthusiasm

- have an open and questioning mind

- come up with interesting new ideas and things to do

- are idealistic

I have trouble with Sevens because they

- don't want to be deprived of any new or fun experience, so they don't always come home when they say they will

- become impatient with me when I ramble

- are often indecisive, as I am

- are self-centered

- have a much faster pace than I do

What Nines Say About Eights (Asserters)

I like Eights because they

- are sensual, passionate, and exciting

- act spontaneously and decisively

- are a good model for me when I want to be more forceful or direct

- are loyal and generous

- think independently and have strong convictions

- encourage me to express my anger

I have trouble with Eights because they

- come toward me like a platoon

- snap at me with no awareness of the impact

- dismiss my opinions

- are too intense and controlling and seem to think the world won't keep going without them

What Nines Say About Nines

I like Nines because we

- understand each other's laid-back style

- both value life's pleasures and comforts

- make each other feel loved and accepted

- are always open to doing what the other wants to do, if only we *knew* what we wanted to do

I have trouble with Nines because we

- want everything to be all right between us and tend to overlook problems that come up

- build up resentments from tolerating too much from each other

- procrastinate

- have trouble making up our minds

Things Nines Would Never Dream of Doing . . .

☞ refusing an invitation to the hot tub or to play golf because they want to get their taxes done a month early

☞ bragging for hours at their reunion about how wonderfully they are doing and not asking others how *they* are

☞ making to-do lists for each day that leave no time for transitions or lounging, then following them exactly

☞ wearing the gaudiest and most attention-getting outfit they can find to meet their new girlfriend's or boyfriend's parents

☞ screaming and insulting their partner at the welcome party they're hosting for their new neighbors

☞ being ignored in a threesome and insisting on receiving all of the attention for the remainder of the evening

☞ deciding they were a Nine immediately after reading this chapter and not wondering if they might be another type

How to Get Along with Nines

- Appreciate their kindness, gentleness, and patience.

- Give them compliments, hugs, and other forms of loving attention.

- Appreciate what they do instead of focusing on what they don't do.

- Be patient when they take a long time to make decisions.

- Be aware that some Nines take a request as an accusation that they haven't done what they were supposed to.

- Be sensitive about giving criticism or asking them to do something.

- "Would you like to . . . ?" or "Would you help me . . . ?" will probably be well received, but they'll gnash their teeth if you say, "Do this!" or "You should do this!"

- Keep in mind that they rebel under pressure, nagging, or complaining.

You can give Nines extra support in these ways:

- Be a good listener. They like to bounce their ideas off someone.

- Encourage them to let their grievances out.

- Reassure them that you will not disconnect from them if they say no. They will often clam up, disappear, or space out rather than risk rejection.

- Help keep their environment peaceful.

- Encourage them to share *their* interests and desires with you rather than always going along with what you and others want to do.

- Help them find out what they want to do or how they feel by asking clarifying questions. Offer them some choices.

- Gently encourage them to prioritize and set goals.

Chuck discovered what he liked doing and developed a successful business. He was known for loyalty to his customers.

THE ACCIDENT

HOW TO GET ALONG
Using the Eight Myers-Briggs Preferences

The Myers-Briggs Type Indicator (MBTI) can help you determine how healthy a potential relationship might be for you and how to deal with the relationships you already have. The more you know about the pitfalls, the better your judgment will be.

We will define the eight preferences and describe how the sixteen MBTI types interact in relationships.

If you have a relationship with someone like you, you might understand him or her more easily and have fewer conflicts. But if you choose to be with your opposite, you'll have the opportunity to take on some of his or her traits that are different from yours and make your personality more whole. Healthy relationships contain a rich combination of similarities and differences.

Extroverts

Fifty percent of U.S. males are Extroverts.
Fifty-five percent of U.S. females are Extroverts.

Extroverts are sociable, talkative, fast-paced, and likely to act first and reflect on it later.

Extroverts like it when you

- show them you appreciate their friendliness, enthusiasm, and ability to initiate activities
- exchange feelings and ideas with them; this is how they become energized and clarify their thoughts
- join them in their favorite activities

Introverts

Fifty percent of U.S. males are Introverts.
Forty-five percent of U.S. females are Introverts.

Introverts are relatively reserved, usually feel most comfortable when alone or with one other person, and are likely to reflect first and act later.

Introverts like it when you

- understand their need to rejuvenate by being alone
- don't pressure them to be sociable or to act more enthusiastic than they feel
- are patient and give them the time they need to respond
- listen carefully when they speak so they don't have to repeat themselves

Friday after work at the Browns'.

Introvert

I can't WAIT to have a quiet weekend!

I can't WAIT to go out on the town!

Extrovert

WELCOME

Sensates

Fifty-five percent of U.S. males are Sensates.
Fifty-five percent of U.S. females are Sensates.

Sensates are realists and tend
to rely on information obtained
directly through their five
senses.

Sensates like it when you

- appreciate their ability to be down-to-earth
  and focus on the present
- explain things step-by-step; it can frustrate
  them when people jump from one thing to
  another or speak in abstractions
- include details, facts, and specific examples
  when talking with them

Intuitives

Forty-five percent of U.S. males are iNtuitives.
Forty-five percent of U.S. females are iNtuitives.

Intuitives (abbreviated by *N*) get much of their
information through hunches, insights, and in-
spirations and think about many possibilities,
not just the information at hand.

iNtuitives like it when you

- appreciate their ability to see the big picture,
  invent new ideas and new ways of doing
  things, and solve problems creatively
- take an interest in what they have to say, even
  about things that don't have a direct, practical
  application
- don't inundate them with details

It amazes me that you can fix a VCR!

Thanks! Now tell me more about philosophy!

iNtuitive

Sensate

Thinking Types

Sixty-five percent of U.S. males are Thinking types.
Thirty-five percent of U.S. females are Thinking types.

Thinking types are relatively impersonal and analytical and are bothered by ineffective reasoning.

Thinking types like it when you

- appreciate their ability to be logical, rational, and clear
- refrain from probing their feelings
- trust them to offer suggestions and advice in order to help you make a decision, and trust that their intention is not necessarily to make a negative statement about you

Thinking-type females may not feel accepted, since they have traits associated with masculinity.

Feeling Types

Thirty-five percent of U.S. males are Feeling types.
Sixty-five percent of U.S. females are Feeling types.

Feeling types focus on people, value tact, harmony, and good communication, and are sensitive to criticism.

Feeling types like it when you

- appreciate their ability to conciliate, sympathize, express feelings, and make others feel comfortable
- express your affection and praise often, verbally and through cards, hugs, and special gifts
- listen to their feelings without trying to solve their problems (unless they ask specifically for advice)
- try to acknowledge and emphasize areas where you agree
- refrain from using sarcasm or caustic wit
- appreciate their sensitivity

Feeling-type males may not feel accepted, as they have traits that are not considered masculine.

Judging Types

Sixty percent of U.S. males are Judging types.
Sixty percent of U.S. females are Judging types.

Judging types are decisive, orderly, tend to be serious, and try to whittle down options and decide quickly.

Judging types like it when you

- appreciate their efficiency and their ability to complete what they start
- don't make last-minute changes or spring surprises on them
- understand their need to be conscientious and to complete their work before they can relax
- are punctual—they hate waiting and wasting precious time

Perceiving Types

Forty percent of U.S. males are Perceiving types.
Forty percent of U.S. females are Perceiving types.

Perceiving types keep their options open while collecting more and more information, tend to be flexible and tolerant, and dislike tight schedules.

Perceiving types like it when you

- appreciate their adaptability, spontaneity, and ability to see many sides of an issue
- do spur-of-the-moment activities with them
- give them time to make decisions
- understand their style of jumping from one activity to another

Judging

Perceiving

The Sixteen MBTI Types and How to Get Along with Them

Traditionalists: The SJ Temperament

Forty percent of U.S. males are Sensate Judging.
Forty percent of U.S. females are Sensate Judging.

Sensate Judgers

- live by shoulds and should nots; they are responsible, dutiful, trustworthy, and loyal, and expect their partner to be the same
- often value commitment, marriage, and family above their individual desires

- are realistic and live by clearly defined roles: males see themselves as protectors and providers, females as caretakers and nurturers
- are usually careful with money
- can worry about unlikely calamities befalling them
- put off relaxing until all their work is completed

SJs may be attracted to the optimistic, spontaneous types, who complement their seriousness but who may be seen later as unpredictable and irresponsible.

ESTJ

Fourteen percent of U.S. males are ESTJs.
Eight percent of U.S. females are ESTJs.

ESTJs (Extroverted, Sensing, Thinking, Judging types) are assertive, straightforward, logical, blunt, active, and decisive. They are sociable but can be quick to find fault with other points of view or strong emotions. They often insist on taking charge, which can be a problem to a partner who wants an equal relationship. ESTJs are often attracted to warm, nurturing, feeling types.

ESTJs are often Eights and Ones, or less often, Threes and Sevens.

ISTJ

Fourteen percent of U.S. males are ISTJs.
Eight percent of U.S. females are ISTJs.

ISTJs (Introverted, Sensing, Thinking, Judging types) are practical, fastidious, well organized, punctual, and often have high expectations of themselves and others. They are loyal, steadfast, and sometimes seen as uncompromising. There is often an attraction between the serious ISTJ and a playful feeling-type partner.

Ones, Fives, and Sixes are frequently this type.

ESFJ

Five percent of U.S. males are ESFJs.
Thirteen percent of U.S. females are ESFJs.

ESFJs (Extroverted, Sensing, Feeling, Judging types) are warm, gentle, and sympathetic. They show their love in practical, helpful ways. They are talkative and gregarious, like to be needed and appreciated, and may sacrifice their own needs for another's. ESFJs often choose a warm, accepting partner (some Nines, for instance) and may feel ignored by someone who is reserved (some Fives, for instance).

Twos and Sixes are frequently this type.

ISFJ

Five percent of U.S. males are ISFJs.
Twelve percent of U.S. females are ISFJs.

ISFJs (Introverted, Sensing, Feeling, Judging types) are usually reserved, patient, gentle, and extremely dependable and loyal; they give a great deal of themselves to others. Accepting help and expressing negative feelings are difficult for them. ISFJs are extremely dutiful and often feel overburdened by responsibilities.

Ones, Twos, and Sixes are frequently this type.

Action Oriented: The SP Temperament

Eighteen percent of U.S. males are Sensate Perceiving.
Sixteen percent of U.S. females are Sensate Perceiving.

Sensate Perceivers

- are fun-loving, optimistic, and spontaneous
- often avoid confinement, obligation, and routine
- crave variety and excitement
- tend to use their money to have a good time rather than to save for a rainy day
- express caring more through action than words
- are sometimes quiet, curious onlookers, especially thinking types
- avoid conflict and may leave a relationship when dissatisfied rather than confront the issues

SPs often choose partners who are stable and responsible and who provide an anchor for their spontaneous, adventurous lifestyle. They appreciate partners who give them freedom to pursue their hobbies
and interests.

ESTP

Five percent of U.S. males are ESTPs.
Two percent of U.S. females are ESTPs.

ESTPs (Extroverted, Sensing, Thinking, Perceiving types) are charming, gregarious, witty, and like
being in the limelight. They are antiauthoritarian and like challenges. Their partners may find them impulsive, restless, blunt, and insensitive and may be forced to take second place to the ESTP's adventurous
activities.

Sevens are frequently this type.

ISTP

Five percent of U.S. males are ISTPs.
Two percent of U.S. females are ISTPs.

ISTPs (Introverted, Sensing, Thinking, Perceiving types) are independent, realistic, and self-determined.
They like adventure and challenge, are often socially indifferent and reserved, and focus their enthusiasm on tools, machines, and things they can do with with their hands.

Fives and Sevens are frequently this type.

ESFP

Four percent of U.S. males are ESFPs.
Seven percent of U.S. females are ESFPs.

ESFPs (Extroverted, Sensing, Feeling, Perceiving types) can be warm, sparkly, energetic, and the life of
the party. They are caring, quick to show affection, and they like to fill their home with people. They live
in the present, find enjoyment easily, and give follow-through a low priority. ESFPs value harmony and
accentuate the positive. Some people find them scattered and hyperactive.

Twos and Sevens are frequently this type.

ISFP

Three percent of U.S. males are ISFPs.
Five percent of U.S. females are ISFPs.

ISFPs (Introverted, Sensing, Feeling, Perceiving types) are reserved, natural, gentle, modest, helpful, and trusting. They express their love and caring by quietly doing things for others. ISFPs have an accepting, live-and-let-live attitude and can be overlooked or easily intimidated by their partner.

Nines are frequently this type, and sometimes male Fours.

Knowledge Seekers: The NT Temperament

Twenty-six percent of U.S. males are iNtuitive Thinking.
Sixteen percent of U.S. females are iNtuitive Thinking.

Intuitive Thinkers

- value their independence and often encourage it in their partner
- like to debate issues and may be competitive and argumentative
- value being logical and rational and are frequently interested in systems
- tend to intellectualize their feelings and avoid discussions about relationships
- dislike overdone or public expressions of affection
- may pursue interests or career goals at the expense of spending time with their partner or family
- may have little interest in social rituals such as anniversaries and birthdays
- can be aloof and detached, especially when introverted

Female NTs often have a difficult time in our culture, since many of their qualities are seen as masculine.

ENTJ

Eight percent of U.S. males are ENTJs.
Five percent of U.S. females are ENTJs.

ENTJs (Extroverted, iNtuitive, Thinking, Judging types) are confident, ambitious, direct, and want to be in charge. They are often a challenge for their partner, for they can be confrontational, quick tempered, and critical. ENTJs are often attracted to warm, nurturing, and adaptable types who complement their controlling personalities.

Ones, Threes, Sixes, and Eights are frequently this type.

ENTP

Six percent of U.S. males are ENTPs.
Four percent of U.S. females are ENTPs.

ENTPs (Extroverted, iNtuitive, Thinking, Perceiving types) are competitive, gregarious, witty, sponta-neous, and usually have a lively circle of friends. They value freedom and independence, like to take risks, and thrive on mental challenges. Their testing nature can be tiring to some. ENTPs are not particu-larly organized and don't always follow through on what they start. They are often attracted to warm, supportive, sensitive types.

Sixes and Sevens are often this type.

INTJ

Seven percent of U.S. males are INTJs.
Three percent of U.S. females are INTJs.

INTJs (Introverted, iNtuitive, Thinking, Judging types) are logical, theoretical, and very independent. They are responsible, loyal, and demanding of themselves. Often reserved and detached, they are sometimes self-righteous and may lash out with criticism. Though they are sensitive to rejection, they will usually retreat rather than show it. INTJs may either choose a partner carefully and rationally or fall hopelessly in love with a partner with whom they have little in common.

Ones, Fives, and Sixes are frequently this type.

INTPs

Six percent of U.S. males are INTPs.
Three percent of U.S. females are INTPs.

INTPs (Introverted, iNtuitive, Thinking, Perceiving types) are reserved, detached, and cerebral. They are often absorbed in their world of books, learning, and thought. Socializing has little appeal to them, though they do like an occasional lively discussion. They have a tendency to be negative, cynical, and argumentative. INTPs are sometimes attracted to nurturing, outgoing partners who can provide some anchor to the outside world. They can feel intruded upon when their partner wants attention.

A very high percentage of male and female Fives are this type.

Identity Seekers: The NF Temperament

Sixteen percent of U.S. males are iNtuitive Feeling.
Twenty-six percent of U.S. females are iNtuitive Feeling.

Intuitive Feelers

- look for meaning in life
- dream of having a perfect, fulfilling relationship
- are empathic and affectionate
- try to bring out their own and their partner's potential
- avoid conflict unless their ideals are violated
- are very sensitive to criticism

Female NF idealists are often drawn to the NT knowledge seekers, who appreciate their warmth, compassion, idealism, and originality. Male NFs have a difficult time in our culture, since many of their qualities are seen as feminine. They may overcompensate by being seductive, overly aggressive, or stubborn and inflexible.

ENFJ

Four percent of U.S. males are ENFJs.
Seven percent of U.S. females are ENFJs.

ENFJs (Extroverted, iNtuitive, Feeling, Judging types) are responsible, energetic, helpful, and enthusiastic. They are good communicators, socially skilled, and like to be with others. ENFJs value commitment, loyalty, and living peacefully. If there is conflict in the relationship, or if their relationship breaks up, they may blame themselves or become spiteful and resentful. They thrive on affection and affirmation and can be disappointed when this is not forthcoming.

Ones, Twos, Threes, Sevens, and Eights are often this type.

ENFP

Seven percent of U.S. males are ENFPs.
Twelve percent of U.S. females are ENFPs.

ENFPs (Extroverted, iNtuitive, Feeling, Perceiving types) are dynamic, spontaneous, fun-loving, enthusiastic, and are seen by some as overly positive. They need affirmation and may become so involved with others that they forget themselves. It seems they are perpetually in love with someone or something new. ENFPs are usually affectionate and can become fickle when their enthusiasms change.

Twos and Sevens are frequently this type.

INFJ

Three percent of U.S. males are INFJs.
Five percent of U.S. females are INFJs.

INFJs (Introverted, iNtuitive, Feeling, Judging types) are determined, responsible, creative, and loyal. They tend to be somewhat reserved and to like solitude. Because of their strong need for harmony, INFJs often fail to assert themselves or set limits and may keep their pain to themselves. They are acutely aware of other people's feelings and become deeply hurt when not understood. INFJs want a partner who understands and accepts their idealism.

Ones and Fours are often this type.

INFP

Six percent of U.S. males are INFPs.
Seven percent of U.S. females are INFPs.

INFPs (Introverted, iNtuitive, Feeling, Perceiving types) are loyal, compassionate, contemplative, and gentle. They tend to be creative, self-critical, and modest and need to have plenty of time alone. They are sensitive to rejection or scorn and may have difficulty sharing their feelings. They look for a soul mate who can appreciate their depth, idealism, and sensitivity.

Female INFPs are often admired for their inner strength and determination, but males may feel disapproved of, by other men especially.

Fours and Nines are often this type.

ENNEAGRAM TYPES AND MBTI TYPES

Expanded from *The Enneagram Made Easy*
by Renee Baron and Elizabeth Wagele, © HarperSanFrancisco 1994

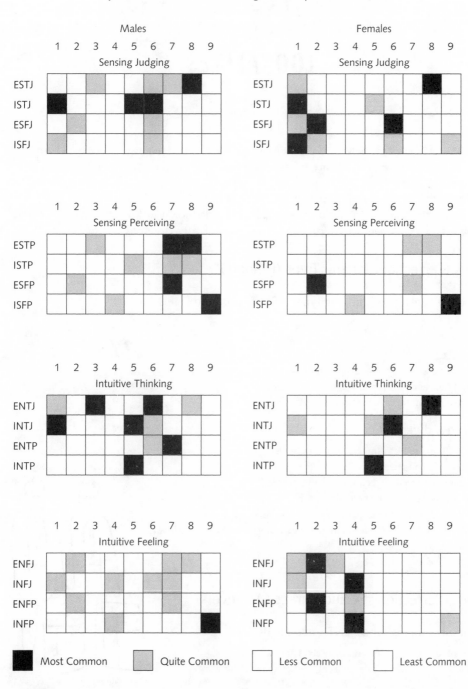

LOOKALIKES

Now that you understand how the two personality systems intersect, you may be interested in some of the finer points of telling Enneagram types apart. This section should help you if you are still uncertain about your type.

When two Enneagram types share MBTI preferences, they are especially difficult to tell apart.

We have indicated the most frequently shared MBTI preferences of lookalike types under the heading of each section. A more detailed comparison can be found in the charts on page 167.

Ones (Perfectionists) and Twos (Helpers)

Especially Feeling and Judging types: ESFJs, ISFJs, and ENFJs

- are helpful, like to give advice, and try to be good
- are self-critical
- tend to worry a lot
- can be controlling, possessive, and self-righteous
- feel hurt and angry when taken for granted
- are reluctant to say what they want or need

How they differ

Ones focus on getting things done the right way.
    Twos focus on relating to other people.
Ones tend to keep their feelings to themselves.
    Twos tend to show their feelings.
Ones tend to set clear boundaries.
    Twos often have unclear boundaries, especially when extroverted.
Ones tend to be skeptical.
    Twos tend to be trusting.

Ones (Perfectionists) and Threes (Achievers)

Especially Judging types: ENTJs and ENFJs

- have high expectations of themselves and others
- are hardworking, active, efficient, and push for closure

- have difficulty delegating responsibility, since they believe no one is as effective as they are
- tend to be conventional and traditional

Feeling-type Ones and Threes are sensitive to criticism and want to please, help, and avoid conflict. Thinking-type Ones and Threes are objective, tough-minded, and more concerned with data and things than with people.

How they differ

(Ones are more likely than Threes to be introverted.)

Ones sometimes have a moralizing quality to their speech.

    Threes sometimes have a bragging quality to their speech.

Ones usually complete one task before moving to another.

    Threes often have several tasks going at once.

Ones tend to do things methodically.

    Threes tend to do things expediently.

Ones tend to be solid, pragmatic, and consistent.

    Threes tend to be charming, charismatic, and can change to fit others' expectations or the situation.

Ones tend to be pessimistic and worry about past and future mistakes.

    Threes tend to be optimistic and focus on their success.

Ones (Perfectionists) and Fours (Romantics)

Especially INFJs

- are idealistic and tend to be dissatisfied with things as they are
- have strong consciences and have high standards for themselves
- can be hardworking and persevering
- are usually refined and dignified
- are self-righteous

How they differ

Ones tend to control their emotions.

    Fours tend to be emotional and let their sadness show.

Ones see strong feelings as threatening or improper.

    Fours value deep or strong feelings.

Ones usually follow and enforce society's rules.

    Fours usually follow their own rules.

Ones tend to be realistic, practical, and down-to-earth.

    Fours tend to be imaginative, creative, and fanciful.

Ones (Perfectionists) and Fives (Observers)

Especially ISTJs and INTJs

- are logical, objective, impersonal, and emotionally controlled
- have high standards and strong consciences

- concentrate well and are self-disciplined
- worry a lot and try not to make mistakes
- are independent and self-reliant

How they differ

Ones tend to be down-to-earth and make practical improvements.
    Fives tend to be abstract and theoretical.
Ones tend to be traditional and follow rules.
    Fives tend to be unconventional and antiauthoritarian.
Ones tend to take an active role.
    Fives tend to stand back and observe.
Ones focus on narrowing options and making decisions.
    Fives focus on collecting information.

Ones (Perfectionists)
and Sixes (Questioners)

Almost all of the eight Myers-Briggs judging preferences occur in both of these types

- have a strong sense of duty and commitment
- tend to be skeptical in the beginning of a relationship and establish trust slowly
- focus on principles and causes
- are often anxious and pessimistic
- tend to overwork and have trouble relaxing
- like clear-cut guidelines, especially when Sensing or Judging
- tend to be sympathetic and helpful (when Feeling types)
- tend to be analytical and confrontational (when Thinking types)

(Ones and Sixes are some of the most difficult types to tell apart).

How they differ

Ones have a grounded quality (as do most people who are in the gut center).
    Sixes have an anxious quality about them (as do most people who are in the head center).
Ones tend to repress or deny anger.
    Sixes tend to show their anger, especially when counterphobic.
Ones behave consistently.
    Sixes tend to behave unpredictably.
Ones are concerned with rules and being right.
    Sixes are concerned with being safe (either by going against authority when counterphobic or by scanning for danger when phobic).
Ones want closure and usually make decisions quickly.
    Sixes want closure too but have trouble with decisions.

Ones (Perfectionists) and Eights (Asserters)

Especially ESTJs, ESTPs, ENTJs

- are hardworking, ambitious, and goal oriented
- can be workaholics
- stand up adamantly for their principles and ideals
- are confident and direct
- can be impatient, argumentative, and insensitive to others' feelings
- take responsibility and inspire others to do the same
- are self-reliant and independent
- tend to see things in black and white

How they differ

Ones are often moderate, well-mannered, and proper.
    Eights can be excessive, insulting, and loud, especially Thinking types.
Ones try to be reasonable.
    Eights sometimes like to shock people and don't mind if people think they are unreasonable.
Ones are methodical and deliberate.
    Eights tend to be spontaneous and fast-paced.
Ones' anger may build until they eventually explode.
    Eights may snap at people and unload their anger right away.
Ones apply steady pressure on others to change.
    Eights often intimidate to bring about change.

Twos (Helpers) and Threes (Achievers)

Especially ENFJs

- are friendly, enthusiastic, sociable, energetic, and articulate, especially when extroverted
- keep track of how people respond to them; try to look good and present a pleasing image
- may hide their vulnerability behind a show of confidence
- like to receive approval, recognition, and admiration
- have difficulty expressing negative feelings directly

How they differ

Twos want to be valued for their generosity.
    Threes want to be valued for their accomplishments and success.
Twos get a sense of self from their relationships with others.
    Threes get a sense of self from their work.
Twos can be overly emotional and dramatic, especially when Perceiving types.
    Threes are relatively restrained emotionally.
Twos like to talk about their feelings.
    Threes like to talk about their goals.

Twos may give up their own interests for another's.

Threes usually stay focused on their own goals.

Twos often like to process their feelings, especially when they move to their Four arrow.

Threes tend to avoid heavy feelings.

Twos (Helpers) and Fours (Romantics)

Especially ENFPs

- are warm, supportive, and compassionate
- place great importance on their relationships and are insightful about people
- are highly sensitive to rejection
- can be dramatic, intense, jealous, and possessive
- seek attention and approval, especially when extroverted
- have strong consciences and suffer from guilt
- are likely to push and pull on their partners
- place importance on self-expression

(Twos and Fours are almost always Feeling types.)

How they differ

(Extroverted Fours are more likely to resemble Twos than are introverted Fours.)

Twos tend to focus on others and try to be upbeat.

Fours tend to be self-absorbed and moody.

Twos try to hide their sadness.

Fours let their sorrow show.

Twos tend to reach out to people.

Fours are often withdrawn, especially when introverted.

Twos express themselves by giving to others.

Fours express themselves through communicating feelings.

Twos (Helpers) and Phobic Sixes (Questioners)

Especially ESFJs and ISFJs

- are warm, friendly, and compassionate
- form deep bonds with others
- try to be helpful and give advice
- are sensitive to criticism
- are eager to be liked and may subordinate themselves to another
- fear abandonment

How they differ

(Twos are not likely to resemble Thinking-type Sixes.)

Twos want people to like them above all.

Sixes want people to protect them above all.

Twos use flattery.

Sixes suspect the motives of those who use flattery, though some use it themselves.

Twos cover up or are out of touch with their anxiety.

Phobic Sixes are all too aware of their anxiety.

Twos need to *feel* right about the decisions they make.

Sixes try to *think* of everything when making decisions.

Twos tend to focus on the positive.

Sixes imagine the worst.

Twos are trusting and, when extroverted, readily invite many people into their lives.

Sixes accept others into their lives only after carefully determining that they are trustworthy.

Twos (Helpers) and Sevens (Adventurers)

Especially Extroverts: ESFPs, ENFPs, and ENFJs

- are outgoing, enthusiastic, entertaining, and fun-loving
- are optimistic and idealistic
- like to motivate others
- seek affirmation from others
- may be charming, seductive, and flirtatious
- are spontaneous (especially when Perceiving)

How they differ

(Twos are usually Feeling types and are not mistaken for Thinking-type Sevens.)

Twos focus on others' lives.

Sevens tend to focus on their own projects and plans.

Twos want people to feel comfortable telling them their problems.

Sevens are often uneasy about listening to others' problems.

Twos want to be needed and indispensable.

Sevens don't want people to be dependent on them.

Twos often give up their own interests for the other's in a relationship.

Sevens are likely to stay with their own interests.

Twos try to be tactful and not offend anyone.

Sevens can be relatively blunt and outspoken.

Twos are in the heart center and strive to make feeling connections.

Sevens are in the head center and try to stave off fear.

Twos (Helpers) and Nines (Peacemakers)

Especially Feeling types

- are empathic, supportive, generous, and trusting
- are warm and cheerful, especially when extroverted
- often have difficulty being assertive and expressing anger

- may depend on others to give them a sense of well-being
- tend to accommodate their partner

How they differ

(Since Twos usually are Feeling types, Thinking-type Nines are not likely to resemble them.)
Twos can be intense and dramatic, especially when extroverted.

Even when extroverted, Nines are relatively reserved, calm, and even-tempered.
Twos usually reveal their feelings easily.

Nines tend to keep their feelings to themselves, especially when introverted.
Twos generally limit their attention to one person at a time.

Nines are apt to merge with any of a large range of things: a person, a group, and so on.
Twos often look self-confident and are concerned with their image.

Nines seem modest and unpretentious.

Threes (Achievers) and Sixes (Questioners)

Especially Thinking and Judging types

- are responsible and energetic, and have high expectations of themselves and others
- are often charming
- are objective, tough minded, and like to be in control
- often overwork and have trouble relaxing

How they differ

Threes tend to focus on their own personal goals or achievements.

Sixes tend to focus on their duty to the cause or the group.
Threes tend to be confident and positive.

Sixes tend to be anxious and pessimistic.
Threes focus on what can be done rather than on what might go wrong.

Sixes tend to mull over mishaps and failures and predict doom.
Threes get things done in the most expedient way possible.

Sixes tend to procrastinate.
Threes can have difficulty working with others because no one is as effective as they are.

Many Sixes derive pleasure from working as a member of a team.
Many Threes tend to avoid confrontation.

Sixes, when counterphobic, are often confrontational.

Threes (Achievers) and Sevens (Adventurers)

Especially Extroverted types: ESTJs, ESTPs, ENTPs, and ENFJs

- are busy, optimistic, and tend to be fast moving and extroverted
- are often charming and seductive; seek admiration and attention
- become anxious around depressed, unhappy, needy, or dependent people

- try not to let their relationship get in the way of their projects and goals
- may withdraw from relationships when they start to become overly intimate
- try to keep things light and can be superficial
- are friendly and helpful, especially Feeling types
- are direct and challenging, especially the Thinking types

How they differ

Threes are always coming up with new goals to work toward.
  Sevens are always making plans for new adventures.
Threes are relatively self-contained and reserved.
  Sevens tend to be uninhibited and impulsive.
Threes tend to be traditional and conforming.
  Sevens are often unconventional and antiauthoritarian.
Threes may have several projects going on at once and push to complete them all.
  Sevens also have several projects going at once but may leave some unfinished.

Threes (Achievers) and Eights (Asserters)

Especially Extroverted types: ESTJs, ESTPs, ENTJs, and ENFJs

- have a lot of energy, strength, stamina, and enthusiasm
- are assertive, ambitious, and may be workaholics
- take responsibility and are often in leadership roles
- like to motivate others
- carry out projects with purpose and passion
- are self-reliant and self-directed
- often hide or deny insecurities, vulnerabilities, and feelings

How they differ

Threes strive for admiration.
  Eights strive for respect.
Threes are relatively traditional and conforming.
  Eights pride themselves on being individualists and nonconformists.
Threes are relatively controlled, contained, and self-disciplined.
  Eights can be noisy, exuberant, and overindulgent.
Threes try to be diplomatic and avoid conflict.
  Eights often like to stir things up and shock people.
Threes try to control how they are seen and can act affected.
  Eights find pretense distasteful.
Threes may try to manipulate people to get them to work hard.
  Eights don't care about being Mr. Nice Guy.

Fours (Romantics) and Fives (Observers)

Especially INFJs and INFPs

- are original, insightful, and creative, especially when iNtuitive
- tend to be unconventional and eccentric
- are hypersensitive to criticism
- are withdrawn and sometimes loners
- are often socially insecure

How they differ

(Thinking-type Fives are not likely to resemble Fours.)
Fours are often emotional and moody.
    Fives seem objective and calm.
Fours try to create drama and intensity in relationships.
    Fives want their relationships to be smoothe and stable.
Fours want to express their feelings and be understood.
    Fives feel awkward about expressing their feelings and often keep them
    to themselves.
Fours become intensely involved with people.
    Fives tend to keep some distance from people, even in intimate relationships.

Fours (Romantics) and Sixes (Questioners)

Especially iNtuitive Feeling types

- are warm and compassionate
- value beauty, aesthetics, and creativity
- question and analyze their own and others' motives and feelings
- fear abandonment
- are supersensitive and easily feel misunderstood
- are prone to feeling guilty or ashamed
- can be intense and hysterical

How they differ

Fours seek relationships that are intense and dramatic.
    Sixes seek relationships that are steady and secure.
Fours trust that what their feelings tell them is true.
    Sixes, even when Feeling types, use their reasoning
    to verify the truth.
Fours usually have calm and sometimes breathy or sad voices.
    Sixes usually have halting or nervous-sounding voices.
Fours lean toward depression.
    Sixes lean toward anxiety.

Fours (Romantics) and Sevens (Adventurers)

Especially iNtuitive and Feeling types

- are imaginative, expressive, and flamboyant when extroverted
- fantasize about having exciting love relationships and make them happen
- vacillate between enjoying being committed and wanting their freedom and independence
- often have discriminating taste in food and clothing
- seek intensity and are nonconforming
- are idealistic and want to contribute something to the world

How they differ

(Thinking-type Sevens do not resemble Fours.)
Fours want to connect emotionally to others and
talk about feelings and relationships.

> Feeling-type Sevens want to connect emotionally
> also but may prefer sharing experiences and
> talking about adventures.

Fours may dwell on the darker feelings and are in touch with suffering and pain.

> Sevens go after happiness and novelty and avoid unpleasant feelings.

Fours are often hard on themselves.

> Sevens usually like and are good to themselves.

Fours often feel uncomfortable and different in groups, even when extroverted.

> Sevens are often at ease in groups.

Fours usually remember having had a sad or lonely childhood.

> Sevens often remember having had a happy childhood.

Fours (Romantics) and Nines (Peacemakers)

Especially Feeling and Perceiving types: ENFPs, INFPs, and ISFPs

- are warm and compassionate
- usually avoid conflict and confrontation
- are soft-spoken and reserved, especially when introverted
- are inclined to be spiritual and like to dream and fantasize, especially when iNtuitive
- can be stubborn and resistant
- are sensitive to criticism
- may have difficulty making decisions, especially Perceiving types

How they differ

Fours are intense and dramatic, especially when extroverted.

> Nines are relatively calm and composed.

Fours often have an offbeat style.

> Nines usually have a rather conservative style.

Fours long for things to be different from what they are.

> Nines tend to accept things as they are.

Fours makes accusations or provoke a fight when ignored.
  Nines will often space out or get lost in other
  activities when ignored.
Fours are attached to their melancholy feelings.
  Nines tend to deny such feelings.

Fives (Observers) and Sixes (Questioners)

Especially Introverted and Thinking types: ISTJs and INTJs

- tend to be competent and knowledgeable
- usually have a good sense of humor
- often play the devil's advocate
- sometimes feel socially awkward and can have difficulty communicating tender feelings
- can be arrogant, cynical, argumentative, and rebellious
- can be paranoid, negative, and alienated

How they differ

Fives are usually soft-spoken, reserved, and withdrawn.
  Sixes are more likely to be sociable, outspoken, and outgoing, especially when extroverted.
Fives behave fairly consistently.
  The behavior of Sixes often oscillates from one extreme to the other.
Fives often look calm.
  Sixes appear nervous or high-strung.
Fives try to appear emotionally detached.
  Sixes, especially when counterphobic, have visibly strong or intense reactions.

Fives (Observers) and Nines (Peacemakers)

Especially Introverted types: ISTJs, INTJs, and INFPs

- try to avoid conflicts and disturbing situations
- are curious: they seek and collect information
- are soft-spoken
- try to look calm and peaceful in order to disguise their fear
- may be passive-aggressive instead of direct with their anger
- can be perceptive and insightful
- look to others to trigger their energy
- often withhold their feelings
- become stubborn when others place demands on them

How they differ

Fives seem aloof from others.
  Nines often merge with others, especially when Feeling types.

Fives tend to be suspicious and cynical.

    Nines tend to be trusting and optimistic, especially when Feeling.

Fives tire of being with others for long periods of time and often isolate themselves.

    Nines often enjoy hanging out with others for long periods of time.

Fives often communicate in a terse and succinct way.

    Nines tend to ramble.

Fives are highly focused.

    Nines are easily distracted.

(Nines often mistake themselves for Fives, but not vice versa.)

Sixes (Questioners) and Sevens (Adventurers)

Especially Extroverted types

- are outgoing, sociable, and often have a good sense of humor
- are often endearing and lovable
- can be blunt, overreactive, authoritarian, and defensive, especially the Thinking types
- are often impulsive, nervous, and manic

How they differ

Sixes like the security of a committed relationship.

    Sevens often keep their options open and avoid commitment.

Most Sixes like predictability.

    Sevens like pleasant or exciting surprises and novelty.

Sixes often control their behavior, especially when phobic.

    Sevens are often uninhibited.

Sixes constantly analyze and doubt people's motivations.

    Sevens aren't overly concerned about hidden agendas and that sort of thing. They mainly hope others want to have adventures with them.

Counterphobic Sixes (Questioners) and Eights (Asserters)

Especially Thinking types: ESTJs and ENTJs

- stand up for truth and justice and defend the underdog
- are loyal and protective
- can be quick tempered, intimidating, hostile, or violent
- often distrust others; see the world as dangerous
- are antiauthoritarian and nonconforming
- can become fearless while taking action or can take action even when terrified

How they differ

(These Enneagram types are among the most difficult of all to tell apart.)

Sixes often yield when pressure is applied.

    Eights may intimidate under pressure.

Counterphobic Sixes take control but may react, maneuver, or take evasive action for their safety.

Eights take control also but are more likely to rule the space around them and to stand their ground.

Sixes may give lengthy explanations or repeat themselves to make sure they are understood.

Eights are blunt and get right to the point.

Sixes, as part of the thinking center of the Enneagram, try to make sure they have thought of every reason why they should or shouldn't make a decision.

Eights, as part of in the gut center of the Enneagram, are likely to make decisions easily and instinctively.

Sevens (Adventurers) and Eights (Asserters)

Especially ESTJs and ESTPs

- are energetic, enthusiastic, and exuberant
- are confident, assertive, and can be aggressive
- are self-reliant and independent
- are often egocentric
- can be impulsive, reckless, and overindulgent
- are antiauthoritarian and test rules

How they differ

Sevens will poke and tease but don't want to create bad feelings.

Eights sometimes promote and thrive on disharmony.

Sevens usually smile a lot and have a demeanor that attracts people.

Eights can look intimidating and sometimes scare people away.

Sevens can be indirect and evasive.

Eights are usually direct and blunt.

Sevens are often mercurial and light, which reflects their head center.

Eights have a solidity about them, which reflects their gut center.

Sevens (Adventurers) and Nines (Peacemakers)

Especially ENFPs

- focus on the positive and tend to be generous, friendly, cheerful, and idealistic
- avoid conflicts and situations that might lead to painful feelings
- enjoy new experiences
- can be stubborn; hate it when people make demands of them
- are often talkative
- are aware of so many options that they have problems making choices

How they differ

Sevens tend to be self-promoting.

Nines tend to be modest and self-effacing.

Sevens seek excitement.

Nines seek contentment.

Sevens usually get what they want, by direct or indirect means.

Nines often don't know what they want and might be reluctant to ask if they knew.

Sevens are likely to escape from difficult or boring situations.

Nines may forget to notice that a situation is not going well for them.

Sevens often initiate activities.

Nines wait for others to take the initiative.

Sevens may be brusque and impatient.

Nines are usually mild-mannered and not in a hurry.

RECOMMENDED READING

Enneagram Books

Condon, Thomas. *The Enneagram Movie and Video Guide.* Portland, OR: The Changeworks, 1994.

Hurley, Kathleen V., and Theodore Dobson. *What's My Type?* San Francisco: HarperSanFrancisco, 1992.

———. *My Best Self: Using the Enneagram to Free the Soul.* San Francisco: HarperSanFrancisco, 1993.

Naranjo, Claudio. *Character and Neurosis.* Nevada City, CA: Gateways, 1994.

———. *Ennea-Type Structures.* Nevada City, CA: Gateways, 1990.

———. *Enneatypes in Psychotherapy.* Prescott, AZ: Hohm Press, 1995.

Palmer, Helen. *The Enneagram.* San Francisco: HarperSanFrancisco, 1991.

———. *The Enneagram in Love & Work.* San Francisco: HarperSanFrancisco, 1995.

Riso, Don Richard. *Personality Types.* Boston: Houghton Mifflin Co., 1987.

———. *Understanding the Enneagram.* Boston: Houghton Mifflin Co., 1990.

———. *Discovering Your Personality Type.* Boston: Houghton Mifflin Co., 1992.

Rohr, Richard, and Andreas Ebert. *Discovering the Enneagram.* New York: Crossroad Publishing Co., 1990.

Myers-Briggs Books

Hirsh, Sandra, and Jean Kummerow. *Life Types.* New York: Warner Books, 1989.

Keirsey, David, and Marilyn Bates. *Please Understand Me.* Del Mar, CA: Prometheus Nemesis Book Co., 1978.

Kroeger, Otto, and Janet Thuesen. *Type Talk.* New York: Bantam Doubleday Dell, 1988.

Myers, Isabel Briggs, and Peter B. Myers. *Gifts Differing.* Palo Alto, CA: Consulting Psychologists Press, 1980.

Relationship Books

Hendrix, Harville. *Getting the Love You Want: A Guide for Couples.* New York: Pocket Books, 1988.

———. *Keeping the Love You Find: A Guide for Singles.* New York: Pocket Books, 1992.

Other Enneagram Resources (Tapes, Books, Publications)

Credence Cassettes, 115 E. Armour Blvd., P.O. Box 419491, Kansas City, MO 64141-6491.

The Changeworks Catalogue, P.O. Box 1066, Portland, OR 97210-0612.

···

ACKNOWLEDGMENTS

Thanks to:

The entire Harper staff for their invaluable help.
Linda Allen, our agent.

For their work on the Enneagram:

Don Riso, Rusty Hudson, Claudio Naranjo, Oscar Ichazo, Richard Rohr, Thomas Condon,
Rich Byrne, Helen Palmer, Michael Gardner, Mani Feninger, Kathleen Hurley, and
Theodore Dobson, and special thanks to Maylie Scott and Tom Clark.

Those we interviewed for our book:

Eve Abbot	Nancy Brown	Will Davis	David Freeman
Claire Achen	Suzanne Buckley	Gita Dedek	Michai Freeman
Karen Adams	David Burke	Monika Delson	Lee Anna Friedman
Gaila Marie Allen	Judy Burke	Penny DeWind	Naomi Friedman
Betty Alvater	Ross Burkhardt	Elena Diena	Holly Fulton
John Argue	Joyce Burks	Susan Donefeld	Renee Gamez
Chris Bailey	Rich Byrne	Christian Eddleman	Harry Gans
Deborah Baisch	Claudia Cadwell	Victoria Eddleman	Key Gardner
Dan Baron	Bonnie Cameron	Ben Eiland	Dori Geller
Jodi Baron	Linda Campa	Annette Evenary	Phil Gerrard
Tami Baron	Elaine Chernoff	Gloria Everett	Nicholas Gerson
Sondra Beck	Mara Chitayat	Sylvia Falcon	Happy Glaser
Joyce Beckett	Glen Chrystal	Shiela Fish	Lee Glickstein
Sarah Berger	Camille Chutczer	Dan Fivey	Landes Good
Eloise Bergesen	Elaine Cleland	Teri Fivey	Dreena Goode
Judy Bess	Michelle Cobb	Jean Flattery	Lloyd Goode
Sam Blood	Sandra Cobb	Fran Foltz	Belinda Gore
Betty Bower	Mano Collinge	Gary Foltz	Linda Grayson
Robyn Brode	David Cook	Randall Fonts	Martin Gross
Bob Brown	Miranda Copty	Janet Forman	Olivia Guthrie
Christopher Brown	Ramy Copty	Ken Forman	Ellen Hage
Corky Brown	Karen Costarella	Rick Foster	Anita Hamm
Lois Brown	Mary Beth Crenna	Sucheta Frankel	Gary Hayes

Kristi Helmecke
Richard Hendrickson
Randi Hepner
Greg Hicks
Ed Hirsh
Joan Hitlin
Lois (Suji) Hochenauer
Maribeth Hudson
Valentine Illitch
Ernie Isaacs
Fred Isaacs
Sikha Isaacs
Marge Jamison
Ken Jenkins
Margaret Jones
Chinabear Joseph
Nancy Kanat
Gary Kaplan
Lori Kaplan
Marci Kaplan
Marilyn Kaplan
Donna Kaufman
Nancy Kesselring
Alma Key
Premseri Khalsa
Shakti Singh Khalsa
Jenny Kolkhorst
Selene Kramer
Stephen Kresge
Kerda Kroen
Steve Kruszynski
Martina Lawlor
Harriet Whitman Lee
Lolli Levine
Emily Lloyd
Ginny Logan

David Luke
Vivienne Luke
Norris Lyle
Ellen Lynch
Howard Margolis
Ellen Margron
Rebecca Mayeno
Karen McArdle
Alison McCabe
Sarah Meyer
Sharda Miller
Diane Mintz
Kan Mondfrans
Ed Mooney
Kailen Mooney
Debby Nakamura
Dennis Nakamura
Judith Nasau
Trevor Nelson
Lianne Obadia
Ellen Odza
Timothy O'Hagain
Peter O'Hanrahan
Carol Olson
David Olson
Wendy Oser
Fran Packard
Sita Packer
Patricia Padgett
Susan Page
Dave Parrett
Karen Paulsen
Dana Paxton
Harry Payne
Yolanda Petersen
Linda Petty

Mary Phalen
Pamela Pitts
Jim Popf
Paula Powers
Ann Price
Sarah Pujans
Cindy Putnam
Scott Ramsey
Nick Raspanti
Chuck Renfroe
Tatini Rider
Gwinn Rigsby
Marlina Rinzer
Shankiri Rise
Tricia Rissman
Gregory River
Peter Rogers
Helga Romoser
Loie Rosenkrantz
Gary Rosenthal
Tom Rosin
Tom Rucker
Patricia Salcido
Lucienne Sanchez-
   Resnik
Beth Sanguinetti
David Sapper
Arlette Schlitt-Gerson
Juditte Schwartz
Kathi Seasons
Jo Sherrill
Vicki Silva-Smith
Liz Simmonds
Steven Smith
Susan Sohrakoff
Rosie Sorenson

Henry Sotelo
Ellen Strong
Bill Swahlen
Duncan Tam
Toni Tischler
Linda Tobin
Frances Torrey
Shirley Towbis
Brent Turner
Ann Tussing
Susan Urquhart-Brown
Bob Valdez
Catherine Valdez
Noni Verbiscar-Brown
Peter Verbiscar-Brown
Robert Volberg
Augie Wagele
Gus Wagele
Martha Wagele
Nicholas Wagele
Charlotte Waggoner
Gloria Wayne
Susan Weinstein
Elin Weiss
Eileen Williams
Maureen Williams
Marlinda Woodberry
Ann Woodward
George Woodward
Steve Woolpert
Gail Wread
Jeremy Yun
Marcie Zellner
Michael Ziegler

....

ABOUT THE AUTHORS

Renee Baron, a writer and therapist who uses the Enneagram
in her counseling practice, and Elizabeth Wagele, a writer and
professional cartoonist, are the authors of *The Enneagram Made
Easy: Discover the Nine Types of People*. Both live in Berkeley, CA.